W9-CGP-222

CANADA

GOOD NEIGHBOR TO THE WORLD

DISCOVERING
OUR HERITAGE

CANADA

GOOD NEIGHBOR TO THE WORLD

BY ADAM BRYANT

DILLON PRESS
PARSIPPANY, NEW JERSEY

Photo Credits

(Photo credits from previous edition)

Photographs supplied courtesy of the following: Clellen Bryant; Mark Bryant; Burlington Northern; Ann Callaghan; Canadian Amateur Hockey Association; Canadian Government; Canadian Public Archives—66 (C 27638); Charles H. Stern Agency; M. B. Ellis; Farm and Country; James Heimann; Imperial Oil Limited; Tim Irwin; Robert Lansdale; Steven Mitchell; Ross Murdy; NASA; © OECA—25 (Ian Sampson), 62, 76, 132 (Jan Sampson); Ontario Government; Ontario Ministry of Agriculture and Food; Ontario Science Centre; Gweneth Pearce; Progressive Conservative Party of Canada; Royal Canadian Mounted Police; George Shane; Toronto Public Library; TV Ontario

(Second edition photo credits)

Front Cover: Map, Ortelius Design. *l.* Adam Bryant, *m.* Royal Canadian Mounted Police, *r.* Tom Stack & Associates/© Thomas Kitchen.

Courtesy, Calgary Stampede: 111. Canada In Stockl Inc./© Jim Merrithew: 104. NBA Photos/Scott Cunningham: 152. Courtesy, Niagara Falls, Canada, Visitor and Convention Bureau: 114. Courtesy, Office Of The Prime Minister, Ottawa, Canada: 89 Photo Researchers, Inc./Suzanne Szasz: 136. Shooting Star International/Ron Davis: 164. SBG: 7. Map, Ortelius Design: 8—9.

Every effort has been made to locate the original sources. If any errors or omissions have occurred, corrections will be made.

Library of Congress Cataloging-in-Publication Data

Bryant, Adam.
    Canada, good neighbor to the world / by Adam Bryant. —2nd ed.
    p. cm. — (Discovering our heritage)
    Includes bibliographical references and index.
    Summary: Discusses the people, geography, history, language, folklore, industry, and customs of Canada.
    ISBN 0-382-39498-4 (lsb) — ISBN 0-382-39612-X (pbk)
    1. Canada—Juvenile literature.   [1. Canada.]   I. Title. II. Series.
F1008.2.B78   1997
917.1—dc20   96-2555

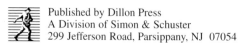
Published by Dillon Press
A Division of Simon & Schuster
299 Jefferson Road, Parsippany, NJ 07054

Second Edition
Printed in the United States of America
10 9 8 7 6 5 4 3 2

CONTENTS

FAST FACTS ABOUT CANADA

Official Name: Dominion of Canada.

Capital: Ottawa.

Location: Canada is the second largest country in area in the world. It occupies the entire northern half of North America (except for Alaska). It is bordered by the Atlantic Ocean to the east, the Pacific Ocean and Alaska to the west, and the Arctic Ocean to the north. To the south lies the United States of America.

Area: 3,831,033 square miles (9,922,330 square kilometers); the greatest distances within the country are 2,875 miles (4,628 kilometers) from north to south and 3,223 miles (5,189 kilometers) from east to west. Canada has 151,490 miles (243,800 kilometers) of coastline.

Elevation: *Highest*—Mount Logan, 19,520 feet (5,950 meters) above sea level; *Lowest*—sea level at the coasts.

Population: *Estimated 1994 population*—27,932,000; *Distribution*—77 percent live in or near cities; 23 percent live in rural areas; *Density*—7 persons per square mile (3 persons per square kilometer).

Form of Government: Parliamentary democracy.

Important Products: *Agriculture*—beef cattle, wheat, milk, hogs; *Fishing industry*—cod, salmon, lobster, scallops; *Fur industry*—mink, fox, lynx, beaver; *Manufacturing*—food products, transportation equipment,

petroleum and coal products, paper products; *Mining*—petroleum, natural gas, natural gas liquids, coal.

Basic Unit of Money: Canadian dollar.

Official Languages: English and French.

Major Religions: Roman Catholic, United Church of Canada, Anglican; minority religions include Greek Orthodox and Jewish.

Flag: Two broad vertical red stripes, which frame a red maple leaf on a white background.

National Anthem: "O Canada."

Major Holidays: New Year's Day—January 1; Good Friday and Easter Sunday; Victoria Day—May 24; Canada Day—July 1; Labour Day—first Monday of September; Thanksgiving Day—second Monday of October; Remembrance Day—November 11; Christmas Day—December 25.

Motto: "A mari usque ad mare" ("From sea to sea").

Floral Emblem: Maple leaf.

GREENLAND
(Denmark)

Baffin
Bay

Davis Strait

Denmark Strait

B a f f i n   I s l a n d

CANADA

NORTH
AMERICA

EUROPE

ASIA

AFRICA

SOUTH
AMERICA

AUSTRALIA

ANTARCTICA

Hudson
Bay

urchill

N E W F O U N D L A N D

★ St. John's

QUEBEC

Gulf of
St. Lawrence

Cape
Breton
Island

Charlottetown
★

PRINCE
EDWARD
ISLAND

NEW
BRUNSWICK

ONTARIO

C A N A D I A N   S H I E L D

LAURENTIAN MOUNTAINS

Fredericton
★

St. Lawrence River

Halifax
★

NOVA
SCOTIA

Quebec City
●

Bay of
Fundy

Lake
Nipigon

Lake of
the Woods

Lake Superior

Ottawa
☆

Montreal
●

North

Atlantic

Ocean

Sudbury
●

Toronto
★

Lake Huron

Lake Ontario

Lake Michigan

Windsor
●

Lake Erie

THE RICHES OF CANADA

Canada is a land of great variety and richness. Its geography includes Arctic glaciers and sunny British Columbia orchards. There is barren northern rock and fertile southern farmland. Such variety shapes the lives of Canadians, who work in deep-sea fishing and coal mining, wheat farming and lumbering, banking and health care.

The many languages and cultures of Canada make life interesting for Canadians and all who visit the country. There are two official languages in Canada: English and French. But many other languages—about 40 in all—are spoken by the rich blend of people who have come to Canada from all over the world. Besides preserving their languages, these immigrants also continue the traditions of their homelands, through cultural festivals, parades, and community celebrations.

Other riches lie in the Canadian wilderness. Minerals are one of these treasures. Not many years ago the world's largest goldfields were discovered in the province of Ontario. The country also has major deposits of zinc, petroleum, asbestos, nickel, and uranium. In addition, Canada has the largest supply of fresh water in the world. The country's countless lakes are used not only for drinking water and sports but also for hydroelectric power.

Canada considers its diverse people one of its greatest riches.

In addition, vast forests cover nearly a quarter of Canada's territory. These trees provide nearly half of all the newsprint used worldwide.

Canada's great size is one reason the country has so much to offer. Canada is the second largest country in the world in area (only Russia is larger). North to south, Canada stretches farther than the distance from New York to Los Angeles. It is so wide that it covers six time zones from east to west. That means there is a six hour time difference from coast to coast!

The Atlantic Coast

Canada is made up of ten provinces and two territories. Its landscape has many faces. In the east, the province of Newfoundland juts far out into the Atlantic Ocean. It is made up of the island of Newfoundland and the coastal region of Labrador. The province is known for its dense forests, rocky cliffs, and sea-weathered towns. Many of the towns on the coast were given funny names by the early explorers, such as Witless Bay and Come-By-Chance. St. John's, the capital of the province, is Newfoundland's largest city.

The Atlantic Provinces—Prince Edward Island, New Brunswick, and Nova Scotia—are mostly wooded highlands. Families in the Maritime Provinces, as this

*Prince Edward Island's scenic coasts and beaches
draw many tourists.*

region of Canada is known, make their living mainly by
forestry, farming, and fishing. Other industries include
tourism, manufacturing, and mining. Many tourists flock
to the beaches of the Maritimes each summer for a seaside
vacation. The colorful provincial capitals—Charlottetown
(Prince Edward Island), Halifax (Nova Scotia), and
Fredericton (New Brunswick)—also play host to
thousands of visitors each year.

To the west and north of the Maritime Provinces is the
province of Quebec. Quebec is Canada's largest province
in area, although its population is smaller than Ontario's.

It is the center of French-Canadian culture. About 80 percent of its people speak French. In fact, Quebec is one of the largest French-speaking communities in the world outside of France. The province's most famous cities, Montreal and Quebec City, the capital, are known worldwide for their lively cultural life and for the quiet charm of their well-preserved historical areas. Situated on the shores of the broad St. Lawrence River, these cities are also busy centers of manufacturing, which is the leading industry in Quebec, followed by agriculture.

Stretching over northeastern Canada is the great Canadian Shield. Shaped like a knight's shield, it covers eight-tenths of Quebec as well as parts of other provinces. The Canadian Shield was actually once a mountain range. But over hundreds of thousands of years, massive glaciers slowly pressed and scraped it into what is now the Shield. The soil is poor for farming but rich for mining. Rivers flowing out of its many lakes supply hydroelectric power for paper mills and other factories. Quebec is also home to the oldest mountains in North America—the Laurentians.

Canada's Heartland

West of Quebec is the industrial heartland of Canada. Factories in the southern part of the province of Ontario make everything from cars to clothes. Americans are often their biggest customers. This region is one of the fastest-growing business centers in the world. At its center is Toronto, home to one out of every eight Canadians. Close to Toronto are other large Canadian cities, including Hamilton, Windsor, and Ottawa, the nation's capital.

The face of Ontario changes dramatically to the north, where thousands of square miles of forest cover the Canadian Shield. People in this region live mostly in scattered towns that grew up around mines or pulp and paper mills. The mills turn the surrounding forests into paper, perhaps the very paper used in this book. The woods are also home to many animals—moose, deer, beaver, wolves, and black bears.

In the middle of Canada, the rocks and trees of the Shield suddenly give way to flat prairies. Outside the cities the horizon is often broken only by a towering oil-drilling rig or grain elevator. The prairies are home to immense farms that provide wheat and other grains to much of the world. They are also home to animals such as the coyote, mule deer, and pronghorn antelope.

The Prairie Provinces include Manitoba, Saskatchewan, and Alberta. In Manitoba, the easternmost prairie province, the main crops include barley, wheat, oats, and flax. But cities like Winnipeg, the provincial capital, have grown so rapidly that manufacturing has overtaken agriculture as Manitoba's leading industry.

A moose grazes in the Canadian wilderness. Many people come to Canada to see its varied and abundant wild animals.

West of Manitoba is the province of Saskatchewan. The great Canadian Shield extends even into the northern part of this province. But to the south lies flatter land, where wheat farms and Saskatchewan's most developed cities, Saskatoon and Regina (the provincial capital), are located.

The Far West

The province of Alberta shares numerous physical features with its prairie neighbors. Its vast flat land in the

The vast farmland of the Canadian prairie in Saskatchewan stretches into the distance beyond a towering grain elevator.

east is used for farming. Manufacturing is also a major industry, carried out in Alberta's main cities, Calgary and Edmonton (the capital). But since the 1960s, mining and oil production have been the focus of Alberta's economy. The province is believed to have some of the richest oil deposits in the world—especially in the Athabasca tar sands.

At the western end of Alberta, the Rocky Mountains rise sharply from the flat land, like an immense wall. The snowcapped Rockies are home to elk and grizzly bear, mountain goats and mountain sheep. These animals often wander near the main highways, where people stop their cars to capture the wildlife on film. Tourists are especially attracted to the province's outstanding national parks— Jasper, Banff, and Wood Buffalo.

The Rocky Mountain range runs all the way from New Mexico to Alaska. In the United States it is divided into the Southern, Central, and Northern Rockies. At the U.S.-Canadian border, the Canadian Rockies start. They extend north into Alaska, where the mountains are called the Brooks Range.

The mountains separate the province of British Columbia from the rest of Canada. This province is famous for its dense rain forests and salmon-rich waters. The climate and land offer special opportunities for people in cities like Vancouver and Victoria, on the Pacific coast.

Beautiful Lake Louise, in Banff National Park, is one of the most scenic places in Canada's Rocky Mountains.

Vancouver's location—among mountains, near rivers, and on the Pacific coast—is ideal for many industries, as well as for outdoor activities.

They can go skiing in the morning on a nearby mountain, and salmon fishing in the afternoon!

The Tundra

To the north of the provinces is a Canada that few people know. It is a land of lakes, rivers, and forests. Very few people live here. In fact, the Canadian government spends millions of dollars every year to find people who get lost in this region.

The northernmost part of Canada is an endless desert of partly frozen land called tundra. This is the Northwest

Territories. Many of Canada's native peoples live here, including about 12,000 Indians and another 12,000 Inuit. (The Inuit, whose name means "the people," were once known as Eskimos.) Another 250,000 people originally from the southern part of Canada also live in the Territories. The cities here, such as Tuktoyaktuk and Yellowknife (the territorial capital), are small.

West of the Northwest Territories is the Yukon Territory, which borders Alaska. Its population is about half that of the Northwest Territories. Many people of the Yukon live in Dawson and the capital city of Whitehorse. The Yukon is sometimes called the Land of the Midnight Sun. In the middle of summer, the sun goes down in the Yukon for only a short time each day. In fact, for a few weeks every summer in the far north, the sun never sets at all! This happens because of the way the earth rotates around the sun and because of the Yukon's location in the far north. The natural beauty of the Yukon attracts many visitors each year. Tourism, though, is just one part of this region's economy. The mining of asbestos, copper, silver, and gold are the principal industries.

Canada's Climate

Many people think of the Northwest Territories and Yukon Territory as cold and icy. But in the summer, temperatures sometimes reach 80° Fahrenheit (27° Celsius). Even though the summer is short, millions of tiny flowers will peep out from between the moss and the rocks before the cold weather returns.

Weather forecasters in the United States often talk about winter storms sweeping out of Canada's north. In many parts of Canada, winters are long and cold. But some people think that all of Canada has that kind of weather in winter. Not true. On the west coast, for example, it rains much more often than it snows in winter. And on the prairies, sometimes a hot dry wind called a chinook comes down out of the mountains. It melts all the snow and gives people a break from winter for a few days.

Southern Ontario has the mildest climate in all of Canada. Its winters are short, and its summers are long. In fact, the southernmost point in Canada—Point Pelee, Ontario—is farther south than parts of California.

Canadian Culture

The culture of Canada is as varied as its land and climate. The oldest cultures in Canada are those of its native peoples—the Inuit and the Indians. Many people also say that Canada has a European flavor. People from France and Great Britain have had a strong influence on life in Canada. Long before Canada became a country, the French explored this part of North America. Like other European explorers in the 1500s, the French crossed the Atlantic in search of a new passage to the markets in the East.

As French explorers traveled deeper into North America, they claimed land for France. Britain also claimed land in what is now Canada. The two countries eventually went to war over this land. Britain won and gained control of what is now Canada. The French were free to stay, and many remained in what is now Quebec. Quebecers today still follow many traditions of their French ancestors, including their system of civil law. The British system of common law is used in the other nine provinces and the two territories.

Governing Canada

Canada reminds European immigrants of their homelands for other reasons. As in Europe, distances are measured in kilometers rather than miles. Temperatures are measured in degrees Celsius, not Fahrenheit, as is common in the United States. Canada's government is also European in many ways.

The national capital is Ottawa, and the center of the Canadian government is Parliament. Canada's parliamentary system is based on that of England. Parliament has a lower house, or House of Commons, and an upper house, called the Senate. Bills become law in Canada after being debated and voted on in the House of Commons and Senate. They must also be passed by the governor-general. The governor-general represents the queen of England, who is the official head of state of Canada, even though Canada became self-governing in 1867. Since the queen rarely visits, her power is exercised by the governor-general. But the head of Canada is really the prime minister, who is the leader of the party with the most elected Members of Parliament in the House of Commons. Under the prime minister is the Cabinet, a group of ministers who head the departments and agencies that provide services to the Canadian public. The prime minister appoints the Cabinet ministers.

The main political parties at the national level are the Progressive Conservative Party, the Liberal Party, the New Democratic Party, Bloc Québécois, and the Reform Party.

Canada's ten provinces have their own governments, each headed by a lieutenant governor. Each province also has a lawmaking body called an assembly. The leader of the assembly is known as the premier. He or she is the head of the party with the most assembly members. The provincial governments have complete control of some areas, such as education. The Yukon Territory and the Northwest Territories are governed mainly by the national government in Ottawa.

Canada's political leaders meet in the majestic Parliament buildings in Ottawa.

Canada and the United States

Canada and the United States are friendly neighbors, but that does not mean that they have not had their share of disagreements. When the United States bought Alaska from Russia in 1867, the U.S. and Canadian governments disagreed over the size of the new state. Their argument was finally settled in an international court. Commerce between Canada and the United States has also caused angry feelings between these neighbors. Each has gone through periods when it has wanted to do more business with the other country. To promote business, one country may decide not to charge taxes on products that cross the border from the other country.

Companies based in the other country may be invited to set up offices in the neighboring country. But Canada and the United States have often changed their minds about such free-trade arrangements, choosing instead to protect their own industries. When trade policies change suddenly, thousands of jobs may be placed at risk and harsh words exchanged between the two countries.

Even though they have argued over free trade, Canada and the United States are still each other's best trading partners. People in the United States buy Canadian products ranging from Nova Scotia lobsters to Ontario-built cars. The leaders of both countries have met often over the years to work out solutions to their joint problems. Their efforts have resulted in a friendship that is among the best in the world. Canada and the United States share the longest undefended border between any two countries.

The United States can consider itself lucky to have Canada as a neighbor. The two countries are alike in many ways. Their people believe strongly in freedom and democracy, for example. But there are also special differences between Canada and the United States. Both countries treasure both their similarities and their differences.

ONE COUNTRY, MANY COMMUNITIES

Canada's name comes from the Iroquois word *Kanata*, which means "village." Canada is like a village or town in many ways, even though it is the second largest country in the world.

Canadians are known around the world as friendly people. Many of them smile at the people they pass each day, whether on a busy city street or on a quiet country road. Another way that Canadians show their friendliness is by welcoming millions of foreigners to make a home in their country. Immigrants to Canada often describe how they were greeted with open arms. And when Canadians travel to other places in the world, they often put a patch on their luggage or clothes showing the Canadian flag. This usually brings a smile from the people they meet.

A word that is often used to describe Canada is *multicultural*, which means "having many cultures." Vancouver, Montreal, and Toronto are three cities that have an especially rich multicultural feeling. For example, the names of streets in these cities are often written in two languages. The particular languages depend on whether you're in Little Italy, Chinatown, or Little Greece! Canadian cities are a perfect place to learn about other

The colorful costumes of these young Canadians reflect the heritage of one of Canada's many cultures.

cultures. You could go to Little Greece in Toronto, for example, and eat souvlaki or moussaka. You could then browse through a Greek bookstore and afterward see a Greek movie. On other days you could "visit" Italy and China without leaving the city!

With so many different cultures, there are also many languages spoken in Canada. In fact, there are too many to name here. Besides English and French, the top eight languages spoken by Canadians are Chinese, Italian, Portuguese, Spanish, German, Punjabi, Polish, and Greek.

Canadians also practice a variety of religions. Most Canadians—about 90 percent of the population—are Christians. Some of the main Christian groups are the Roman Catholic Church, the United Church of Canada, and the Anglican church. But the many people who have made Canada their second home have also brought their religions with them. It is not unusual to pass by the churches and temples of religions such as Judaism, Buddhism, Sikhism, Hinduism, Islam, and the Baha'i faith.

Canadians have helped strong ethnic communities grow. They want everyone to share the music, books, dances, and movies of their homelands. Because of the manner in which their nation was formed—settled at different times by different groups with different aims and goals—Canadians sometimes say of themselves that they do not really have a unified national outlook. One group or another often will feel that its needs are being ignored or its goals pushed aside. Considering how many groups there are, this is not surprising.

Someone once described Canada as a mosaic. A mosaic is a piece of art made up of different-colored bits of stone, glass, or metal that are fitted together to form a single picture. Each "piece" of the country's people, keeping its own heritage alive, helps make up the picture that is Canada.

Canadians Expressing Themselves

Developing a rich culture is important to Canadians. Many donate a great deal of time and money to the arts. The Canadian government also helps the arts thrive through agencies such as the Canada Council and the Arts and Culture branch of the national government. In all, these agencies spend more than 6 billion dollars each year on arts and culture.

Canadians also show their support for the arts by encouraging young people to express themselves. There are excellent schools across the country where children can learn to be dancers, artists, actors, and musicians.

One such school is located in the Rocky Mountains of Alberta in a small town called Banff. Only 7,750 people live in Banff. But in the summer the town is swamped by

Banff's beautiful setting is often an inspiration to the young students at the School of Fine Arts.

some 50,000 tourists who come to see the majestic mountains and the wild animals that roam freely through the national parks. They also come to go to school.

Every year, hundreds of Canada's most talented students of drama, music, and art attend the Banff School of Fine Arts. The Banff School has some of the best teachers in Canada and the most modern equipment. But many students say the best part of their experience is the breathtaking scenery and crisp, fresh air, which make them feel especially creative.

Another great Canadian school for music is actually many schools. *Jeunesses Musicales du Canada* ("Young Musicians of Canada") runs music camps in Quebec, New Brunswick, and Ontario for children of all ages. The school was founded in Quebec by a man who wanted to help young musicians learn their craft.

The National Ballet School, in Toronto, is one of the best schools in the world for young dancers. Besides practicing ballet, students also attend classes in other subjects, such as history and math. That way, they can learn how to dance and get a good education, too. The school's many graduates include two of Canada's most famous ballerinas, Karen Kain and Veronica Tennant.

Art schools such as these play an important role in developing Canadian culture. But not all great Canadian artists learn their craft in a school. Canada's native people, for example, learn and pass their artistic skills on to their children without the help of schools. The beautiful paintings and soapstone sculptures made by the Inuit people of the north are bought and collected by art lovers all over the world. The art of the Inuit usually shows simple scenes from daily life, such as a mother, father, and baby huddled together. It also portrays hunting scenes, such as a man killing a seal. The respect that the Inuit have for animals and their often harsh northern environment can be seen in their art.

Other Canadian painting can also be said to have a particular style. That style has come partly from the work of seven artists: Frank Carmichael, Lawren Harris, A.Y. Jackson, Franz Johnston, Arthur Lismer, J.E.H. Macdonald, and F.H. Varley. Together they are known as the Group of Seven. Like most Canadians, they loved the outdoors. They began to paint together in the 1920s and would often walk into the woods with their paints and canvases. When they found the right spot, they would paint the scene, often with bright colors. During their careers they painted hundreds of stunning portraits of the Canadian wilderness.

Paintings by the Group of Seven hang in many of Canada's 1,700 galleries and museums, including the McMichael Collection in Kleinburg, Ontario, just north of Toronto. The McMichael gallery looks like a huge log

The soapstone sculptures of Inuit artists often show scenes from everyday life in Canada's far north.

cabin and is surrounded by 100 acres of deep woods. In the fall the colors of the leaves outside are as breathtaking as the paintings inside. Many families spend a whole day there, going through the gallery in the morning and then walking through the woods in the afternoon. In winter, some families even bring their cross-country skis.

Canadian Writers

Writing is also an important art in Canada. Since the early days of settlement, writers have expressed their feelings about what it means to be Canadian. In French and in English, authors have written about many aspects of Canada, including its wilderness, family life, and history.

Canadian writers have created many characters that are well known to American readers. *Anne of Green Gables*, by Lucy Maud Montgomery, was first published in 1908. It tells the story of a young orphan girl with a busy imagination who wins the hearts of everyone she meets. *Anne* has been translated into 15 languages and twice has been made into a film. A musical version of the story has played every year since 1965 in Charlottetown, Prince Edward Island.

Another famous character from early Canadian writing was created by Thomas Chandler Haliburton. His hero, Sam Slick, first appeared in the book *The Clockmaker; or the Sayings and Doings of Samuel Slick, of Slickville.*

The book was so popular that it had as great an effect on American humor as it has had on Canadian.

Margaret Laurence is considered one of the most famous Canadian writers. She was born in the town of Neepawa, Manitoba, and began writing stories when she was just seven years old. As she got older, she wrote about the area of western Canada where she grew up. Laurence also wrote many books for children, such as *The Olden Days Coat* and *A Christmas Birthday Story*. Her works are much loved in Canada, and they have been translated into many languages.

Another one of Canada's most widely read authors is Farley Mowat. His books have been translated into 23 languages and are read by people in 40 different countries. Many of his books talk about the beauty of the Canadian wilderness and the danger of spoiling it. One of Mowat's most popular books, *Never Cry Wolf*, is read by many students in the United States and was made into a popular movie. Mowat also has a great sense of humor and has written many children's books. Favorites are *The Dog Who Wouldn't Be* and *Owls in the Family*, which is about his childhood in Saskatoon, Saskatchewan.

Perhaps the best-known writer in Canada is Pierre Berton. He is famous for his Canadian history books, but he is also a journalist and a well-known television personality. Berton was born in 1920 in Whitehorse, which is in the Northwest Territories. His father was a goldseeker during the Klondike Gold Rush, and Berton later wrote a book about that time, called *Klondike*. He has also written two books about the building of the Canadian Pacific Railway across Canada, titled *The Last Spike* and *The National Dream*.

Another popular writer is Mordecai Richler. His best-known book is *The Apprenticeship of Duddy Kravitz*. Most Canadian students read this book in high school. It is the story of a young, energetic Jewish boy growing up around St. Urbain Street in downtown Montreal. It too became a popular movie. Other famous Canadian writers include Margaret Atwood, Alice Munro, and the late Robertson Davies.

Canadian Theater and Music

Montreal is often called the cultural capital of Canada. But the French Canadians of Montreal and the rest of Quebec have had to work hard to keep their culture alive. In recent history they have been outnumbered by non-French-speaking Canadians, but they have long wanted to be recognized as equal. In 1969 the Official Languages Act was passed, making French the second official language. All over Canada, government workers must be able to speak both French and English.

Language is just a part of the culture of French Canadians. Beginning in the late 1960s, many Quebecers joined a movement aimed at strengthening their cultural and political independence. These people wanted French Canadians to have equal rights with English Canadians in cultural, political, and economic affairs. During the 1970s, French-language music, theater, and writing flourished in Quebec. Today the strong belief in preserving Quebec's culture is reflected in the arts of the province, and that passion has resulted in exciting contributions to Canadian culture.

Live theater thrives in Quebec. Some months, there are more than fifty theater productions in Montreal at one time. Most of the plays are performed in French, but occasionally theater troupes from other cities, such as New York, come to Quebec. They know they will be playing to an audience that loves theater.

Theater lovers from the United States often travel to the charming Ontario town of Stratford (named after William Shakespeare's home in England) for the Stratford Festival. For six months every year, the best actors and actresses in the country perform the plays of Shakespeare as well as musicals and contemporary plays. The festival is exciting and features top-notch talent.

If you have ever heard someone speaking French, you know it is a very musical language. The words flow

A young Canadian musician plays the violin.

together very naturally, and there is a rhythm to the sentences. Not surprisingly, all types of music are popular in Quebec. Many French-speaking musicians have achieved success outside the borders of *La Belle Province*, or "The Beautiful Province"—another name for Quebec.

Fans of the opera in New York City will recognize the name of Quebec-born Wilfrid Pelletier. He was a conductor of the Metropolitan Opera of New York. He also made a great contribution to music in Canada and, during the 1960s, was national chairperson of the Jeunesses Musicales du Canada. In popular music, Robert Charlebois and Andre Gagnon are both well known all over Canada and in some parts of the United States.

Other Canadian musicians have been very successful both at home and in the United States. The singers Bryan Adams, Neil Young, Joni Mitchell, Gordon Lightfoot, Bruce Cockburn, k.d. lang, and Raffi are popular across North America.

Reaching Out

In a country as large as Canada, many people live far from cultural centers such as Montreal or Stratford. In the early 1900s the government realized that people in remote areas might feel left out of the country's rich culture. To give all parts of the country a sense that they were part of one community, the government set up a television and radio service called the Canadian Broadcasting Corporation, CBC for short. Established in 1936, the CBC has done remarkably well. Almost all Canadians can receive television and radio programs through the CBC. The CBC even runs a program called the Northern Service for both native and English-speaking people living in the far north. Besides the CBC there is also Radio Canada International, which is shortwave radio. People around the world rely on this service to keep in touch with the news. It is broadcast in eleven languages.

Canada reaches out to the world in other ways. It has played host to EXPO, the world's fair, twice. The first Canadian EXPO, in 1967, marked the one-hundredth anniversary of Canadian self-government. The theme was "Man and His World." More than 50 million people from all over the world came to EXPO '67.

In 1986, Vancouver hosted another EXPO. More than 45 nations took part in EXPO '86, which highlighted the theme "World in Motion—World in Touch." There were more than 60 pavilions showing great adventures in the history of transportation and communications.

Canadians tried to create a feeling of world peace at these fairs. In fact, many Canadians believe their country can make its best contribution to the world in the role of peacemaker. Canada is not a powerful military force like the United States, but Canadian politicians have accomplished a great deal in the campaign for world peace. One leader who made tremendous contributions in this area was Lester B. Pearson, the Canadian prime minister between 1963 and 1968.

Pearson played a key role in the development of the United Nations, which is now based in New York City. The U.N. was set up to keep peace throughout the world. It is also a place where countries can work together to solve the many problems that face the world. Pearson also helped to found NATO, the North Atlantic Treaty Organization. NATO brings together the United States, Canada, and many countries in Europe. Like the U.N., the NATO countries work together to solve any problems they may have. Lester Pearson also played an important role in ending the 1956 Arab-Israeli war, for which he received the 1957 Nobel Peace Prize.

Helping out in dangerous situations is something of a Canadian tradition. Canadians have long been known as courageous and calm in the face of danger. For example, Canadian Ken Taylor became a hero in the United States in what became known as the "Canadian Caper." In 1980 the U.S. embassy in Iran was seized by Iranian rebels. They kept 66 embassy workers prisoner. Six Americans fled to the Canadian embassy, where Taylor, who was Canada's ambassador to Iran, hid them for over two months. On

January 28, 1980, he arranged a daring escape plan for the six, letting them use Canadian passports. With Taylor's aid, they got out of Iran. For his help and courage, Ken Taylor was heartily thanked by both the United States and Canada.

Another key figure in the world peace movement was former prime minister Pierre Elliott Trudeau. In a number of trips during 1983 and 1984, he visited leaders of several countries. Trudeau thought that countries should talk about lowering the number of nuclear arms in each country, to help bring about peace in the world. He was awarded the Albert Einstein Peace Prize for his efforts.

Images of Canada

The world has learned much about Canada through its leaders. For many people worldwide, these leaders are Canada. Most of the country's 27.9 million people are not as famous, but they are just as Canadian.

Canada is the fisherman who sits alone for hours inside his ice-fishing hut atop a frozen lake, playing a waiting game with the fish. A thermos of hot coffee helps keep him warm as he huddles over the hole he has cut in the ice. No matter what the weather, people all over Canada enjoy the outdoor life.

Canada is the family hunched over a bowl of popcorn on a Saturday night as they cheer for their favorite team on

People gather to watch the changing of the guard in front of the Parliament buildings. The guards are just one image of Canada.

Hockey Night in Canada—a long-standing tradition for many families. A passion for sports, and especially for hockey, is shared by many Canadians, young and old, male and female.

Canada is the community softball league, where boys and girls of many backgrounds cheer their teammates under the glow of a setting summer sun. Teamwork is important to the success of a softball team as well as to a country.

Canada is the proud guards who stand watch in front of the majestic Parliament buildings in Ottawa. Buildings old and new tower behind them, reflecting Canada's respect for its history and its enthusiasm for tomorrow. Many Canadians think hard about how Canada should approach the future and look to the past for guidance.

Out of Canada's history have come the country's two national symbols—the maple leaf and the beaver. Like Canadians, there are many different types of maple trees. Depending on the species, they can be large, medium-sized, or small. And like Canadian society, the maple leaf has many colors. The maple tree is noted for its year-round beauty, but it is especially beautiful in autumn when the brightly colored leaves bring cheer to darker days. Because it is so impressive, the maple leaf has become a symbol of Canada and appears on the Canadian flag and in the Canadian coat of arms.

The other official symbol of Canada is the beaver. The beaver was chosen by King Charles I because it is hard-working and its pelt was valuable to early Canadians who traded beaver furs. Canadians have accepted the beaver as a symbol of intelligence, courage, creativity, and determination—qualities that are displayed by people all over Canada who work to contribute to their great nation and the world in which they live.

THE FIRST FRONTIERS

Canadians are fortunate in many ways. They enjoy a rich cultural life and one of the highest standards of living in the world. Some people say that Canadians are also lucky because they never had to fight a war for their independence. That is true, but there were many struggles in Canada's history. In fact, the story of Canada begins with one kind of struggle: the struggle of people against the wilderness.

Canada's first people, now called the Inuit, came from Siberia about 35,000 years ago. They followed herds of bison, mammoths, and caribou across a huge land bridge that once joined Asia and North America. Eventually, they formed tribes and worked together to survive in the harsh wilderness. Today the language of the Inuit reveals the respect they and their ancestors developed for nature. The Inuit have 100 names for snow. But they do not have a word for war. Since surviving in the Arctic is a battle in itself, they could never afford the energy to battle one another. Cooperation, not conflict, was the rule.

The Inuit populated small scattered communities throughout the Arctic, from Alaska to Greenland. Today there are eight main tribal groups: the Labrador, Ungava, Baffin Island, Iglulik, Caribou, Netsilik, Copper, and

In many places towns have replaced the traditional villages of the Inuit people. The Inuit were the first people in North America.

Western Arctic Inuit. They speak a common dialect known as Inuktitut. From those first settlements in the north, some of Canada's native peoples moved into other regions of Canada and became divided into many Indian "families," such as Algonquian and Iroquoian.

The Earliest Visitors

The Vikings were the first people to come to Canada from Europe. Leif the Lucky (Leif Ericsson) and his crew sailed from Greenland to what is today Newfoundland in the year A.D. 1000 and eventually set up several North American settlements. Relics from their first settlement, including cooking pots and part of a ship, can be seen at a place called L'Anse aux Meadows in northern Newfoundland. The Vikings eventually abandoned their North American settlements—no one knows why.

The second group of visitors from Europe were probably Basque sailors from northern Spain and southwest France. They came to Canada in the early 1400s to hunt whales off the coast of Labrador. They did not stay. It would be the English and the French who would eventually come to stay in Canada, over a hundred years later.

In the fifteenth century the kings and queens of Europe began to look for a new route to the markets of the Far East. John Cabot, an Italian navigator, was one of many explorers who wanted to be the first to find that route. Like Christopher Columbus, he thought China could be reached by sailing west across the Atlantic. Cabot got money for his voyage from King Henry VII of England and from English merchants who liked his idea. Cabot and his crew of eighteen men set sail from Bristol on May 2, 1497.

Fifty-two days later, Cabot sighted land. He knew he had not reached China, so he called the unknown place Newfoundland. He claimed the land for England. When he returned to England, Cabot had no riches from the East, but he did give reports of rich fishing grounds. The king was not impressed, but the merchants were.

Cabot returned the following year with five ships and a larger crew. No one knows for sure what happened to him and his crew. He was never heard from again.

The Explorations of Jacques Cartier

When the king of France heard about Cabot's trip, he wanted a Frenchman to be the first to find the passage to Asia. In 1534 he sent Jacques Cartier in search of a route. Cartier sailed across the Atlantic and into the St. Lawrence River. He claimed the land around it for France. When Cartier returned to France and told his king about all he had seen in the new land, the king agreed to finance a second voyage. On his second voyage, Cartier came across

*Jacques Cartier, the French explorer, made three voyages to
North America in the mid-1500s.*

an island on the St. Lawrence with a large hill. He named it *Mont Royal*, which means "royal mountain." Cartier also gave Canada its name. Cartier asked Iroquois Indians he had met what they called their region. They pointed to a nearby village and said, "Kanata." *Canada* is believed to come from this Iroquois word, which means "village." The French applied the word to the surrounding area and later to the whole country.

In 1541, Cartier made a third voyage to North America, this time with five ships and a larger crew. Cartier and his men suffered through a harsh winter and went home in the spring. The king no longer believed Cartier's stories of a passage to the Far East or of the riches in Canada. The French did not try to settle again in that faraway land for another 60 years.

Although the French did not settle in Canada at this time, French ships continued to visit the region to catch the abundant fish in its waters. To keep the fish they caught from rotting on the return voyage to Europe, the crews dried the fish on racks set up on the Canadian coast. While there, they began trading manufactured goods such as kettles, knives, and fishhooks for furs that the local Indians had obtained.

Europeans used the fur as trimming on clothes. When hatmakers discovered that beaver fur made a fine felt needed for men's top hats, they created a great demand for the fur. The hats were so popular and the demand for beaver fur was so great that the king of France decided to encourage settlements in Canada so that the fur trade could be organized and become steady.

New France

Pierre de Gua (a businessman) and Samuel de Champlain (a young mapmaker) were leaders of a group of French who came to settle on St. Croix Island near present-day Maine. With the help of the local Micmac Indians, the French survived their first harsh Canadian winter. The following spring, they moved and established the first successful French settlement. It was called Port Royal, in what is now Nova Scotia.

As Champlain grew more confident, he decided to establish another settlement in what is now Quebec City. (Today, Quebec City is North America's oldest city.) To keep his men happy during the long winter, Champlain founded a club, The Order of Good Cheer (in French, *L'Ordre de Bon Temps*). Each week the men held a banquet with a parade and ceremonies. After dinner they sang, danced, and played games. The Micmac Indians often joined the celebrations.

The French were not the only newcomers to North America. Explorers like Martin Frobisher and Henry

Hudson were still trying to find a passage to Asia. And to the south the English were establishing colonies in what is now the United States. The two groups became trading partners. The French gave the English colonists furs and livestock and received sugar, brandy, and manufactured goods in return.

Soon a struggle between the French and the English began. Both wanted to control the profitable fur trade with the Indians. The French controlled the river routes. They had built trading posts around the Great Lakes at places they named Detroit, Duluth, and Des Moines. The English, meanwhile, were trading west from their colonies and inland around Hudson Bay. They had begun the Hudson's Bay Company in 1670. This fur-trading company would soon be granted vast territory in the north of Canada.

War broke out between the French and the English in 1689. The English had the help of the Iroquois, and the French were supported by the Huron and Micmac. Both sides made savage attacks on each other's settlements. Fighting continued for many years until the French and the British signed the Peace of Utrecht, in 1713. In the agreement the French gave Newfoundland, Acadia (now Nova Scotia), and the region around Hudson Bay to the British, while keeping their territory around the St. Lawrence River and the Great Lakes.

This treaty set the stage for one of the great tragedies of North American history. The French who had settled in Acadia, known as Acadians, felt the land was their home. When they refused to swear loyalty to the British, 8,000 of the original 10,000 French settlers were put aboard ships and sent to Louisiana. Families were sometimes split up during the move, and many never saw their family members again. In Louisiana the exiles became known as Cajuns.

The Battle of Quebec

The peace that followed the Treaty of Utrecht did not last long. The French remaining in Canada were surrounded. To the north lay the English-owned territories of the Hudson's Bay Company. To the south were the British colonies. To the east was Acadia, now owned by the British. In 1756 the Seven Years' War, or French and Indian War, as it was known in North America, began. The British attacked the great stone fortress of Louisbourg on Cape Breton Island, in Nova Scotia. The French defenders of Louisbourg were outnumbered five to one, but they managed to fight off the British for a while. After seven weeks, however, Louisbourg was surrendered. The British now controlled the entrance to the St. Lawrence River, the lifeline of New France. Their next target would be Quebec City, the capital of the French colony.

New France was weakening rapidly. Ships that once came up the St. Lawrence could no longer get food to the French colonists. Bread was rationed, and farmers were forced to kill their horses for food.

Louis Joseph Montcalm was the commander of all the French forces in Canada. Because of the heroic efforts of the French soldiers who defended Louisbourg, Montcalm had time to build up the forces at Quebec City.

Montcalm's British opponent in North America was General James Wolfe. Wolfe hated the French. For the whole month of August in 1759, he had his men burn French farms and houses surrounding Quebec City. The city itself was built at the base of a cliff on the north shore of the St. Lawrence River. Because of its location, Quebec was thought to be safe.

On September 13, 1759, just before sunrise, Wolfe and his army climbed to the Plains of Abraham on the cliff above Quebec City. The French general, Montcalm, had not expected the British to attack from that direction. There were only 100 French troops stationed at the top of the cliff.

As soon as Montcalm learned the English were going to attack, he assembled 3,500 men. The British waited at the top of the hill. They stood their ground and fired as the French came forward. The first and second volleys from the British killed many of the French troops. The battle was over in 15 minutes. Both Montcalm

Quebec City was thought to be safe from attack. But the British climbed the cliffs around it and defeated the city's French defenders.

and Wolfe were killed. In three years, Canada would be entirely in the hands of the British.

Britain Takes Over

The British turned out to be kind conquerors. They soon passed laws allowing the French settlers to keep their language, their form of government, their Roman Catholic religion, and their way of life. It was a wise decision. The British would soon need the French settlers' help, because trouble was brewing in the British colonies to the south.

The British wanted their colonies to the south to help pay for the Seven Years' War, and so they put heavy taxes on tea, sugar, molasses, and other goods. The colonists angrily refused to pay these taxes. They would eventually declare their independence from Great Britain, and they would also try to take Canada away from the British.

In November of 1775, during the American Revolution, an American force captured Montreal. The government there was forced to flee to Quebec City. A second American army attacked Quebec City in the winter of 1775–76. The army was led by Benedict Arnold.

The siege of Quebec City lasted through the long, cold winter. In spring a British fleet came and drove the

Americans away. Benedict Arnold was very surprised that his plan had failed. He had expected the French Canadians to join the Americans against the British. But the French wanted Canada to remain a separate country, and so they stayed neutral during the invasion.

The outcome of the American Revolution affected unsettled parts of Canada to the north and the west. Fur traders from Montreal had bought their furs from parts of North America that were now part of the United States. After the American Revolution they needed to find new sources for their fur. In 1784 they formed the North West Company, which hired explorers to search out sources for furs in the Canadian wilderness. Samuel Hearne, Alexander Mackenzie, Simon Fraser, and David Thompson, along with many friendly Indian guides, such as Matonabbee and English Chief, helped open the Canadian Northwest and West.

The North West Company directly challenged Hudson's Bay Company, which for years had had all of the Canadian wilderness to itself. As they competed with each other, they established systems of trading posts and sponsored adventurous explorers who mapped new areas of Canada. Eventually, the two companies would merge, but their competitive adventures into unknown territory helped settle Canada all the way to the Pacific Coast.

Trouble to the South

As a British colony, Canada was determined to remain separate from the United States. This determination would be tested several times in the years after the American Revolution. One of the first times was when the United States and Great Britain went to war in 1812. The Americans hoped to win the war and take over Canada.

General Isaac Brock was the leader of the British forces in Upper Canada (now Ontario). His army had only 1,300 troops. But Brock won the support of Tecumseh, the great Shawnee chief, who added 600 warriors to Brock's forces. The Shawnee warriors helped Brock win a surprising victory.

When General Brock found out the Americans were planning an attack on Canada, he decided to strike first. The Canadian army and its Indian allies met a large American force and pushed it back to Fort Detroit. Brock told his soldiers to make as much noise as they could to make the Americans think they were a huge army. The plan worked. The following day 2,300 American soldiers surrendered to Brock's smaller force at Fort Detroit without firing a shot!

But the Americans still wanted to control Canada. Over the next two years, several battles were fought along the border between Canada and the United States. By 1814, though, the fighting was over. The Canada-U.S. border had not moved one inch. Never again would the Americans try to take over Canada by force.

Responsible Government

Canadians now had time to shape their country. In 1791, what was then Quebec had been divided into French-speaking Lower Canada and English-speaking Upper Canada by the British Parliament. In each colony the citizens elected an assembly, but the real power was in the hands of the governor (who was appointed by the British king) and a council of rich merchants.

People in both colonies felt this system was undemocratic, and in 1837 they rebelled. In Lower Canada, Joseph Papineau led an uprising, and in Upper Canada the rebellion was led by William Lyon Mackenzie. Both rebellions were quickly put down by British troops, but the message to Britain was clear. British politicians were concerned that another revolution would break out in North America. They agreed to give the Canadians responsible government, or the right to govern themselves. Canada would still be part of the British Empire but would run its own affairs. The British also wanted to make Canada a united country, in case the Americans ever attacked again.

Canadians very much wanted their independence. They also saw the benefits of uniting. But first they had to

The men who worked out the agreement that united the separate colonies in the Dominion of Canada posed for this picture during their 1864 conference.

consider their differences. The smaller colonies of New Brunswick and Nova Scotia were afraid that they would lose all local control. And people in Lower Canada wanted to keep their French language, laws, and education system, and the Roman Catholic religion.

Canadian leaders gathered for a series of meetings. There were many disagreements, but each issue was eventually worked out in what has been called the great Canadian compromise. Part of their solution was that each province in the new Confederation would have its own government, but that the national government would run the army and other services necessary for the whole country.

The agreement was hammered out by John A. Macdonald, George Cartier, Samuel Tilley, Charles Tupper, George Brown, Frederic Carter, John Gray, and others. The Fathers of Confederation, as they are called, listed their agreements and sent them to be passed by the British Parliament. These resolutions became the British North America Act—Canada's written constitution.

A royal proclamation set July 1, 1867, as the first day of the new Dominion of Canada. Canadians were finally united and were about to enter a new and exciting era.

Piecing Together the Mosaic of Canada

On July 1, 1867, Canada became a self-governing country. Canadians threw a huge birthday party for their new nation. There was music, dancing, the best food the land could offer, and many speeches about Canada's promising future. Canadians also cheered for their first prime minister, John A. Macdonald.

Many consider Macdonald the father of Canada, much as Americans think of George Washington as the father of their country. But Macdonald was different, because he worked with Britain rather than rebelling against it. Britain's Queen Victoria knighted him Sir John.

Sir John A., as he was sometimes called, once said, "I had no boyhood. From the age of fifteen, I had to earn my own living." When he was only nineteen, Macdonald opened his own law office. His greatest gift was that he understood people. This ability would be tested often as he worked to build a nation with people determined to keep their traditional ways.

His first test was not long in coming. The new Dominion, or Confederation, of Canada was made up of four provinces: Quebec, Ontario, New Brunswick, and Nova Scotia. Almost as soon as Nova Scotia entered the

Confederation, many people in the province wanted to get out. Nova Scotia was prosperous on its own, and people there thought being a part of Canada would only cost them money. While Canadians celebrated on July 1, 1867, some Nova Scotians hung black flags in their windows.

Joseph Howe was the leader of the Nova Scotian protesters. He went to the British government in London to ask permission for Nova Scotia to leave the Confederation. He was told no. Joseph Howe felt defeated. But Macdonald did a smart thing. He explained to Howe his vision of Canada's future and offered Howe a position in his Cabinet. Howe accepted, and Nova Scotia remained in the Confederation.

Macdonald's next challenge would involve the United States. Even after Canada became a self-governing country, many Americans wanted Britain to give them Canada. At the very least, they wanted the west coast of British Columbia, another British colony, so that they would have a handy link with Alaska. Some American politicians coined the slogan "Fifty-four forty or fight." They wanted the territory that stretched to the fifty-fourth parallel and forty degrees north latitude—the southern tip of the Alaskan panhandle.

Macdonald was in an awkward position. Canada was still a part of the British Empire. The British refused to give away Canada or the west coast, but they wanted peace with

*Sir John A. Macdonald was the first prime minister of Canada
and led the country for over twenty-five years.*

the Americans. So they agreed to many other American demands. The Americans were given free use of the St. Lawrence River and fishing rights in many Canadian waters. Macdonald did not like the agreements. But he knew it was important for Canada to remain at peace with its much larger and more powerful neighbor.

Expansion to the West

With only four provinces, Canada was still a small country. Macdonald was eager to settle the vast and wild land west of Ontario before American settlers could move in. That land was owned by the Hudson's Bay Company, which called it Rupert's Land after Britain's Prince Rupert. Macdonald wanted the Hudson's Bay Company to sell the land to Canada. After much bargaining, Rupert's Land was sold to Canada in one of the greatest land deals in history. The Canadian government gave the company 300,000 pounds sterling, or $1.5 million, for the territory. Canada renamed the land the Northwest Territories.

But not all the land west of Ontario was wilderness. On the Pacific coast, British Columbia, a British colony founded in 1858, had been booming with the gold rush. Thousands of men, many American, had swarmed into the colony to pan for a fast fortune in gold. When the gold ran out, most prospectors left British Columbia. The people who stayed knew they could not remain separate and would have to join a larger country.

But which country would they choose? They decided Britain was too far away, and not enough people supported the idea of joining the United States. In the end, they chose Canada.

But first, British Columbians tried to make a deal with Sir John A. Macdonald. They would join Canada *if* the government would build a cross-country road so that they could feel part of the Canadian family. Macdonald went one step further. He promised them a railway.

The idea of a cross-country railway excited Canadians in both the East and the West. It was a huge task for a country with so few people. Macdonald could have made it easier by choosing a route that went south of Lake Superior into the United States. But he insisted instead on a more expensive and more difficult route, an all-Canada route through nearly a thousand miles of forest and rock in northern Ontario, across the prairies, over the Rocky Mountains, and into Vancouver, British Columbia.

Riel and the Métis

The railway builders were laying tracks across the rugged wilderness when Sir John A. faced his next challenge: trouble on the prairies.

The Rockies presented an enormous challenge to the builders
of the trans-Canada railway.

After Canada bought Rupert's Land from the Hudson's Bay Company, the government sent surveyors to map the new land. That upset the Métis who were living there. The Métis were mostly descendants of fur traders and their Indian wives. They had developed a unique lifestyle based on hunting buffalo and farming, and they were worried that other settlers would ruin their way of life. When the surveyors started mapping the land, the Métis sent for the best-educated man among them, Louis Riel. When Riel arrived, he told the surveyors, "You go no farther." The stage was set for a conflict.

Riel wrote to Sir John A. Macdonald in Ottawa stating his demands. He wanted the Métis to have a say in Parliament and control over their own affairs. But above all, he wanted to keep alive the Métis' way of life. Macdonald wrote back and said the demands were fair. But then Riel made some serious mistakes.

The trouble began in 1869 with a man named Thomas Scott. Riel had set up a separate local government at the Red River Settlement, where the city of Winnipeg now stands. Thomas Scott caused a lot of trouble at the settlement, and Riel put him in jail. He was charged with taking up arms against Riel's government. Found guilty, Scott was executed by a small firing squad.

The news of Scott's death outraged people in Ontario, where he was born. They wanted Riel hanged for Scott's murder. The people of Quebec, however, defended Riel. They blamed the Red River trouble on the people of Ontario, who they said were trying to take away the rights of the French-speaking Métis. To restore order, Macdonald sent soldiers to the Red River Settlement to arrest Riel. Riel fled to Montana.

In 1885, trouble broke out again near the settlement. The Métis were fighting with government soldiers. Riel returned to help his people and led them in a small war known as the North-West Rebellion. The Métis were greatly outnumbered. Riel was captured and taken to Regina, Saskatchewan, for one of the most important trials in Canadian history.

The court decided Riel was guilty of the murder of Thomas Scott 16 years earlier. Riel was ordered to be hanged. It was up to Sir John A. to approve the sentence or spare Riel's life. He knew that whatever decision he made, Canadians would be divided over the issue. In the end, Riel was hanged. Quebecers were outraged at Macdonald, and their anger would last for many years.

The Last Spike

Meanwhile the railway builders had been pressing on, laying track across the prairies and through the Rocky

Mountains. On November 7, 1885, after an almost superhuman effort, a special chapter in Canadian history was completed. At Eagle Pass in Craigellachie, British Columbia, the famous "Last Spike" of the Canadian Pacific Railway was driven. The country was now linked from sea to sea. One of the early passengers was Mrs. Agnes Macdonald, the prime minister's wife. She was a daring woman—she once rode through the Rocky Mountains on the train's cowcatcher, the fan-shaped bumper on the front of the train's engine.

The North-West Mounted Police followed the railway's push into the West. These men in red coats were the main reason that Canada never had major Indian wars or a lawless Wild West like the United States. The Mounties enforced the laws strictly but fairly. There are many stories of a single Mountie commanding the respect of miners, Indians, and settlers who might otherwise have made trouble. Their name was later changed to the Royal Canadian Mounted Police. The RCMP, with their bright red uniforms and shiny riding boots, are now one of Canada's national symbols.

Back in Ottawa, Macdonald was busy with another side of nation building: the economy. American goods at the time were cheaper than Canadian goods. Macdonald wanted to keep American goods out of the country to encourage Canadian business. To do this, he put an extra

The Royal Canadian Mounted Police went west with settlers
in the 1800s and kept order in new communities.
They are a national symbol today.

tariff, or charge, on goods coming in from the United States. He called this the National Policy.

When the economy took a turn for the worse, many people blamed Macdonald's National Policy. The leader of the Liberal party, Wilfrid Laurier, said the trade barriers with the United States should be dropped and replaced with a free-trade policy called reciprocity. Under this policy, neither Canada nor the United States would be taxed when selling goods in the other country.

An election was called in 1890. At that time, Sir John A. Macdonald was seventy-five years old. He won, but the campaign had weakened him. The following year he suffered a heart attack. Newspaper headlines said only: "He Is Dying." Every Canadian knew who "he" was. Sir John A. Macdonald died on June 6, 1891. The nation mourned.

Wilfrid Laurier

Wilfrid Laurier won the next election and became the first French-Canadian prime minister. His childhood had prepared him well for politics. As a young child, Laurier spoke only French. But when he was eleven, his father sent him to an English-language school. He learned to speak English fluently. His ability to understand both English and French points of view would be his greatest strength as a leader of Canada.

Like Sir John A. Macdonald, Laurier was determined to settle the West. He sent officials to Britain to pass out pamphlets with pictures of wheat fields and new homesteads. They took out newspaper ads offering free land to all immigrants. People from Britain started pouring into Canada. Canadian officials also went to Europe to attract skilled farmers from the Ukraine, Poland, and Germany. Since Eastern Europe's winters were often very cold, the officials figured that immigrants from these countries could survive the harsh Canadian winters.

Laurier's campaign to settle the West was a great success. More than two million settlers came to Canada in the early 1900s. Among them were half a million Americans who were attracted by the free land and in return were happy to live under the British Crown.

Laurier once said that the nineteenth century belonged to the United States, but "the twentieth century belongs to Canada." During his first years in power, Canada prospered. That time would be known as the Golden Age of Laurier.

Prime Minister Laurier also was determined to bring about free trade with the United States. He negotiated a treaty of reciprocity and proudly presented it to the voters in the election of 1911. His opponents claimed that reciprocity was a sellout to the United States. Their election slogan was "No Truck or Trade With the

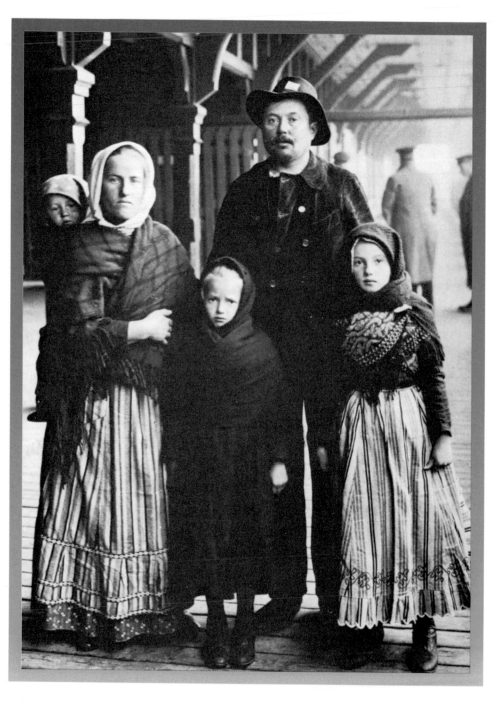

Trainloads of settlers from foreign lands moved to the Canadian west.

Yankees!" Laurier lost, and the Conservatives, the party of Sir John A. Macdonald, took over again.

World War

All the problems at home would soon be set aside because of the situation in Europe. When World War I began, in 1914, Canada was still part of the British Empire—and therefore was automatically at war on Britain's side against Germany.

At the start of the war, Canada had a regular army of only 3,110 soldiers and 684 horses. But Canadians reacted quickly to the crisis. In two months, 30,000 Canadian soldiers were on their way to Europe. That was three years before the United States entered the war. In all, more than 600,000 Canadians served overseas.

Canada's contribution to the "Great War" was remarkable. Canadians took pride in being frontline troops for the British Empire. When other troops retreated from German poison-gas attacks, Canadians held the line. Nearly 25,000 Canadians served in the Royal Flying Corps, the British Air Force.

Several Canadian pilots became heroes. Captain Billy Bishop shot down 72 German planes. And a Canadian pilot, Captain Roy Brown, shot down the most famous German fighter of all—Baron Manfred von Richthofen, the

Red Baron. A Canadian soldier, John McCree, served in a part of Belgium called Flanders Fields, where he wrote the well-known poem "In Flanders Fields."

English Canadians were united by the war. But very few French Canadians volunteered to fight. The French Canadians said they did not feel a part of the crisis in Europe. Besides, the Canadian army used only the English language, as did the Canadian government.

Needing more soldiers for the front lines, the government passed the Military Service Act in 1917. This act allowed the government to conscript—or draft, as Americans say—all single men from eighteen to sixty years of age, whether they wanted to go to war or not. Almost 50,000 new recruits were raised. But conscription added to the bitterness that the French Canadians felt toward English Canada.

The war also changed Canada's relations with Britain. Canada contributed so much to the war effort that the Canadian government demanded more say in the British Empire's affairs. After the war, Canada signed the Peace Treaty of Versailles as a nation in its own right, no longer just a part of the British Empire.

Mackenzie King

After the war, Canadians enjoyed the booming prosperity of the 1920s. A new prime minister was on the scene who would be the central figure in Canadian politics for the next quarter of a century. His name was William Lyon Mackenzie King. Mackenzie King was a clever politician. He had three main aims: to stay in power for a long time, to keep the country united, and to make Canada finally independent of Britain. He succeeded in all three.

Mackenzie King was replaced as prime minister during most of the 1930s, the time of the Great Depression in Canada and around the world. But he was prime minister when Britain declared war on Germany on September 3, 1939. Mackenzie King waited for a week before declaring war on behalf of Canada. It was his way of saying that Canada had gained the right to make its own decisions. Once committed, though, Canada made an enormous contribution to the war effort.

At home, Canadians built ships and planes. They trained pilots from every country in the British Commonwealth. Farmers increased grain production to ship food to Britain. Canadian sailors in ships called corvettes (smaller versions of destroyers) escorted convoys across the Atlantic through waters patrolled by German submarines—a very dangerous task.

In Europe, Canadians fought with strength and courage. Almost 100,000 Canadian men and women died in service. When the war finally ended in 1945, Canadian soldiers had won the respect of the world.

The war moved Canada out of the farming age and into the industrial age. In fact, when the war ended, Canada was one of the strongest nations anywhere.

But in one way, Canada was not stronger. During the war, conscription caused more problems for Quebec. Many French Canadians again saw no need to join in what they regarded as Britain's war. Remembering the problems caused by conscription in World War I, Mackenzie King had promised not to conscript unwilling soldiers again.

But the number of volunteers started to drop soon after the war began. In order to keep up the war effort, King called a special vote, a referendum, asking the Canadian people to let him take back his promise. A huge majority of English-speaking Canadians voted in favor. Men were again recruited without choice. Unwilling recruits were hardly ever sent overseas, but conscription caused bitter feelings among French Canadians toward the rest of Canada.

The Postwar Boom

At the end of the war, in 1945, Canada began "reconstruction." Canadian factories switched from building warships and planes to producing peacetime goods. American companies invested in Canadian industries to develop oil and other resources. During the 1950s, Canadians enjoyed the greatest boom in their history. This happened under Mackenzie King's successor as prime minister, Louis St. Laurent, who ran Canada like a business.

But not everyone shared in the wealth. People in the Atlantic Provinces (which included Newfoundland after it had joined the Confederation in 1949) felt left out. Many people on the prairies felt the same. Neither area had booming industries. Others thought the St. Laurent government was selling Canada's natural resources to the United States.

A fiery politician from Saskatchewan named John Diefenbaker then defeated the Liberal party of St. Laurent to become prime minister. Diefenbaker said he spoke for the people against the big businesses of central Canada. He raised the incomes of people who farmed and fished and spoke of his vision of a developed north.

Canadians felt strongly both for and against Diefenbaker. They were divided almost evenly at election time. The government was on a seesaw during the 1960s, as Diefenbaker and a new Liberal party leader, Lester Pearson, battled for power.

Pearson was an agreeable diplomat. He had won the Nobel Peace Prize when he was Canada's Minister of External Affairs and had helped settle the 1956 war in the Middle East. Pearson eventually became prime minister,

In the 1950s many of Canada's natural resources, such as oil, were developed, and many provinces prospered.

but he never really fired up Canadian voters. He did manage to get everyone to agree on the maple-leaf flag in 1964. Canada had never had a flag of its own—it had always used the Union Jack, the flag of Britain.

Pearson also helped to develop social welfare programs, which benefit many Canadians today. Canadians are protected by unemployment insurance that gives them money when they are out of work. Families receive an allowance or "baby bonus" from the government to help pay for the expenses of raising children. The Canada Pension Plan that Pearson introduced helps support retired people. Pearson also improved medical and hospital insurance for all Canadians.

In the 1960s the face of Canadian politics started to change. A third major party—the New Democratic Party, or NDP—was founded to compete with the Conservative and Liberal parties. The NDP was committed to protecting the rights of workers and to reducing the gap between rich and poor Canadians.

"Masters in Our House"

Changes were also taking place in Quebec, where Quebecers were awakening from what they later called the long night. Ever since they had been defeated by the British in 1759, Quebecers had kept to themselves. They left the world of business to English Canadians. As a result, there were fewer job and education opportunities for French speakers. In the 1960s, Quebecers took action. They changed the leaders of their provincial government and started to insist on being *maître chez nous*—"masters in our house."

Many Quebecers wanted greater independence from the national government in Ottawa. One way they showed this feeling was to create "Quebec House" in Paris, which was almost like an embassy. The Quebec government also took over some businesses in the province. Quebecers insisted that if business people wanted to work in Quebec, they would have to learn French. As their movement grew, their bitter feelings against English-speaking Canadians again came to the surface.

Some Quebecers wanted to go even further and make Quebec a separate country. A few violent separatists put bombs in mailboxes in Montreal. They also kidnapped and murdered a provincial cabinet minister, Pierre Laporte. More responsible separatists formed a political party, hoping to take Quebec out of the Confederation by winning a vote. They named their party the Parti Québécois. Its leader was René Lévesque, a popular television journalist.

Opposing the Parti Québécois was Prime Minister Pierre Elliott Trudeau. Trudeau was a French Canadian like Lévesque, but he was devoted to keeping Canada together. To persuade Quebecers to stay in the Confederation, he offered them a deal: an equal share in all of Canada. That deal changed the lives of many Canadians. Government workers in Ottawa had to learn French. New road signs in both languages were made. Many television and radio stations across Canada started broadcasting in French.

In 1976, René Lévesque became premier of Quebec. He liked to call himself prime minister of Quebec. Lévesque offered a plan known as Sovereignty Association. According to the plan, Quebec would be separated from the rest of Canada, and Quebecers would have total control over their own affairs. When a vote was taken, the majority of Quebecers indicated that they did not want to separate from Canada. Separatism was costing them jobs. Some English-speaking people and businesses were leaving Quebec. But the separatist movement continued. In 1995 the residents of Quebec voted again on whether they wanted their province to be independent of Canada. In a very close vote that stirred strong feelings among people across the nation, those who wanted Quebec to remain part of Canada won once again.

Trudeau also addressed Canada's constitution, which was still in the hands of the British government. He succeeded in getting the provinces to agree on changes that were needed. Changes in the Constitution would no longer have to be approved in Britain.

This was a great accomplishment. But Trudeau was not as successful in other areas, such as the economy. Canada had come to depend on the economy of the United States. Americans owned most of Canada's oil, mining, and manufacturing. Canadians complained that the future of their country was being decided in Dallas and New York. In response, Trudeau set up the Foreign Investment Review Agency to screen all new American investment. He created the National Energy Program to encourage Canadians to become more involved in the oil business. He also set up a government-owned oil company, Petro-Canada.

But there was a price for Trudeau's policies. Many American businesspeople started feeling unwelcome. They stopped investing in Canada. The Canadian economy slowed, jobs grew scarce, and the Canadian dollar dropped in value. When Trudeau retired from politics, Canadians were ready for a change.

Free Trade

The next leader to take and keep power was Brian Mulroney. When he was elected prime minister, his Conservative party won more seats in Parliament than any party had before. His smooth speaking style and ability to win the people's trust brought him a landslide victory.

Mulroney worked to develop Canada's friendship with the United States. His meetings with U.S. president Ronald Reagan led to several agreements, including a deal to tackle acid rain. Acid rain results when certain chemicals from factory pollution become part of the atmosphere. The chemicals later fall to Earth with rain, killing trees and destroying the ecology of lakes. The U.S.-Canada agreement, reached in 1986, was an important step.

Mulroney's economic policies sparked a great deal of discussion and debate. The government attempted to cut the huge national debt left behind by the government under Trudeau by raising taxes. This move made many Canadians angry. It also slowed the economy, because Canadians had less money to spend. In the slower economy there was less work and fewer jobs. Unemployment became a problem in many provinces.

Problems such as unemployment prompted Mulroney to pursue a free-trade deal with the United States. It is often said that history repeats itself. The free-trade issue is a good example. Free trade with the United States has been debated since the Confederation. Sir John A. Macdonald set up trade barriers. Wilfrid Laurier tore them down and pushed for free trade. Many years later, Pierre Elliott Trudeau worked to make Canada more independent of the

United States. When Mulroney took office, he announced, "Canada is open for business again." In 1986, during Mulroney's time in office, the U.S. Senate gave the go-ahead to President Reagan to work out a free-trade deal with Canada.

Free trade continues to be an important but controversial issue for Canadians. The Canadian elections of 1988 were fought over the issue of free trade with the United States. Many people were bitterly opposed to free trade, including a politician named John Turner, who feared that Canada would give up too much to its much bigger neighbor to the south. He warned that free trade would be the "Sale of Canada Act."

Other Canadians leaders also had doubts about increasing trade with the United States. When Jean Chretien took over as prime minister, in 1993, he was opposed to many parts of a proposed broader trade agreement that included not only the United States but also Mexico.

But a year after the agreement was signed, Canada found that it had benefited greatly. Hundreds of thousands of jobs were created as more Americans and Mexicans bought Canadian goods. Canada became the fastest growing of the seven leading industrial countries.

Canada still does not want to become too dependent on the American economy. But Canadians are a confident

Prime Minister Jean Chretien came into office in 1993.

people, certain they can overcome economic problems and
other difficulties that arise. Their confidence has developed
over the course of their history as Canadians have risen
to fight abroad and deal with the stresses and strains at
home of keeping a country as large as Canada together.
Canada has developed from several colonies into a
well-respected, united nation, a country honored for its belief
in multiculturalism and admired for the harmony of the
mosaic of its people.

5

CANADIAN FOLKLORE

Canada's Inuit people and many Indian tribes have passed down hundreds of legends through the generations. The settlers who came to Canada from Europe also brought their own stories. It is easy to understand why Canada's folklore is among the richest in the world.

For Canada's native people the animals and landscape of the Canadian wilderness have long been a source of wonder. They created legends about certain animals and land features.

The Mackenzie River is one of the world's longest waterways. It flows northwest 1,120 miles from Great Slave Lake, in the Northwest Territories, winding through towering mountains on its path to the Arctic Ocean. A famous legend about the river is told by the Slavey Indians of the area.

The legend says that long ago no river flowed from Great Slave Lake, and the lake was much bigger than it is today. At one end of the lake lived a giant, who was as tall as a pine tree. His clothes were made of huge elk skins sewn together, and he carried an immense spear.

One day the giant went out hunting. He had not eaten in a long time, and he was hungry. After a while he found the house of Beaver—a huge beaver from the days of old.

The giant broke down the house. The mother beaver and her young ran out.

The giant killed the young cubs, but Mother Beaver swam across the great lake to escape. The giant ran along the shore, chasing her, until they reached the other end of the lake. Then Beaver came up to a great wall of rock. She gathered all her strength and dug a hole in the rock. With the giant approaching, she quickly pushed herself through and escaped to safety. But the water followed her and created a huge river—the Mackenzie.

Spirits of the Wilderness

Canada's native peoples have a great respect for the Canadian wilderness. Many Inuit stories teach children never to lose this respect. One of these stories tells about the smoking mountains of the Horton River, in the northwest corner of the Northwest Territories.

When the world was very young, the story goes, the first human beings were never alone, because they were always surrounded by spirit people. These spirit people were very much like human beings, but they were invisible. The spirit people liked their human friends and took care of them.

Whenever the northern people were traveling and wanted to pitch camp, the spirit people would begin to

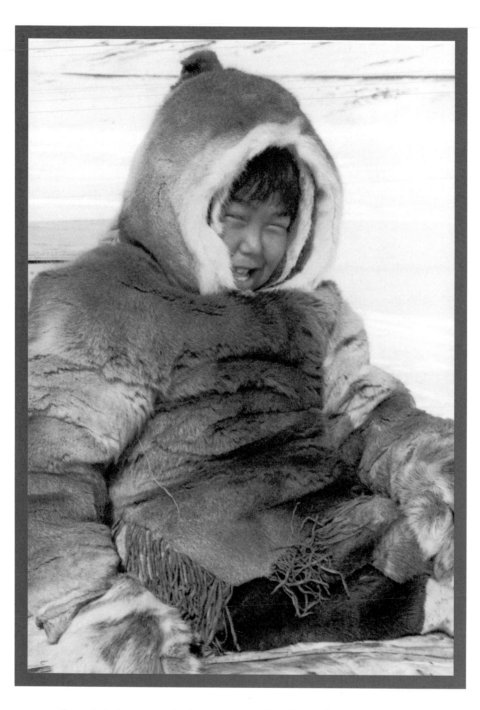

Canada's Inuit people have many tales about the vast, awesome world in which they live.

build snow huts for them. Invisible hands piled the snow blocks together into snow houses.

But one day during a stop in a journey, one of the humans seized his knife and cried out, "What do we want with these people who are always right on our heels?" With these words he shook his knife in the air and thrust it in the direction of the snow huts that seemed to be making themselves. No one heard a sound, but everyone saw the knife become covered with blood.

From that moment on the human people saw no sign of the spirits. Never again did they see the wonderful sight of snowdrifts forming themselves into snow huts when they made camp. They had lost their silent, invisible guardians forever. The spirits had disappeared inside the mountains. There they lived, to escape from the one who had mocked them and wounded their feelings.

That is why, the story says, smoke comes from the mountains near the Horton River. The smoke is from the fires inside, where the spirit people do their cooking.

A Man and His Calf

Settlers from France who made their home in Quebec also brought stories. Many of these stories have a strong religious theme. Many carry a message about honesty and the way people act. "The Calf Sold Three Times" is a funny example of this kind of story.

The story goes that there was a villager who spent all his money on drink, until all he had left was his calf. Since he had no money, he decided to go out and sell his calf.

The first person he met was the village doctor. "Well, friend, won't you buy my calf this morning?" the villager said to the doctor. "How much?" "One gold coin." "Done." The doctor paid for the calf, but he had to go see a patient. He asked the villager to deliver the calf to his farm.

The villager continued on his way with the calf and met one of the town officials. "Well, friend, won't you buy a fine calf this morning?" he asked the official. "How much?" "One gold coin." "Done." Since the official was also on his way to some business, he told the villager to take the calf to his farm.

The villager continued walking along with the calf and met one of the town's lawyers. He said to him, "Well, friend, won't you buy a fine calf this morning?" "How much?" asked the lawyer. "A gold coin." "Done. Take him to my home, for I have to go to another village on pressing business."

The villager went to the next town and stopped at a tavern. He spent all the money he had gotten for his calf.

When the doctor, the town official, and the lawyer returned to find that the villager had not delivered the calf, they decided to arrest the dishonest man. The villager was allowed to get a lawyer of his own and told him his story. The lawyer said, "Your case, sir, is very difficult to defend. Your dishonest act is too clear. However, there's one way of winning this case. Each time that the judge or prosecutor asks you a question, answer by saying, 'Oink, oink, oink!'"

And so when the villager's trial came up, the judge asked the villager, "Sir, have you sold a calf to the doctor here?" "Oink, oink, oink," replied the villager. "Also to this town official?" "Oink, oink, oink." "Is it the same calf you sold to the lawyer?" "Oink, oink, oink." "But did you deliver the calf to these gentlemen?" "Oink, oink, oink." "Why didn't you deliver what you sold?" "Oink, oink, oink." After many more questions, the judge finally said, "You see, sirs, that this man is crazy. I order that he be let go in peace."

After the trial, the villager's lawyer said to him joyfully, "Now that I've won your case, you can pay me for my work." "Oink, oink, oink," was the answer the villager gave. "See here, it's ten dollars, and I'm not going to beg you to pay me." "Oink, oink, oink." "See here, you can't pull that crazy stuff on me. It's I who have won for you." "Oink, oink, oink." "See here, must I get angry to make you pay?" "Oink, oink, oink." And the defending lawyer, just like the doctor, the town official, and the lawyer, got no satisfaction!

Tall Tales

The western provinces of Canada, such as Alberta and Saskatchewan, are famous for their cold winters. Naturally many people tell stories about the cold, trying to describe the coldest weather they can imagine and to tell a story that tops everyone else's. For example, there is the story about the farmer whose words froze. One cold morning in winter, a farmer went to his back door to holler for his pigs. It was so cold out that when he yelled, his words froze in the air. His pigs didn't come home until they heard his words in the spring—when the words thawed out!

One man tells the story about cooking vegetables in the winter. He said that one winter it was so cold that the vegetables and water on the side of the pot nearest the door were frozen while the other side was boiling!

Because there are so many freshwater lakes in Canada, fishing is a favorite pastime for many Canadians. Usually the first question that anglers are asked is, "What did you catch?" Well, there's a story about a woman named Miss Lou Neilson, who used to run a hotel in Cardston, Alberta. She was an excellent fisher, one of the best in Alberta. One time she came home soaking wet, without her canoe. A friend asked her, "Lou, where's your canoe? What happened?"

Miss Lou answered, "I lost the biggest fish I ever caught in my life. It weighed at least 100 pounds. I was

After a day fishing, this couple will have their own fish story to tell.

about 300 yards from shore when I got a bite on my line. As the huge beast came to the surface, it suddenly flipped its tail, upsetting my canoe. I was thrown into the water. Luckily I held on to the line, and when the fish rose again, I slipped the line through its mouth. Then I straddled the huge monster and rode him back to shore!"

The friend asked Miss Lou why she hadn't brought the fish home with her. Miss Lou answered, "Would you have killed the fish that saved your life?"

Sea Legends

When Canada's first cities on the east coast were growing, much of their business came from seagoing ships that carried goods across the Atlantic. People in places like Nova Scotia's Cape Breton Island began to tell stories about the sea. If you ever travel there, you might hear the famous legend of the Phantom Ship.

People say the Phantom Ship appears every now and then off the coast, near the town of Port Hood. It usually happens late at night. All of a sudden the wind comes up, and the weather grows cold. When they look out their window, they are frightened to see a ship, with all its riggings, burning furiously. The sails are on fire, and they fall from the ropes. The masts, too, go down in a shower of sparks. Then the lonely, fire-filled ship drifts into the night and disappears, not to be seen again for years.

As you can see, Canadian folklore is entertaining, and it also offers insights into the lives of Canadians across the country.

CELEBRATIONS OF MANY HERITAGES

Canadians celebrate their heritage all year long. The Canadian calendar is full of holidays that recall events from Canada's past. In addition, all through the year and in all parts of the country, there are festivals of every kind imaginable.

The people who have come to Canada from other countries are encouraged to celebrate their favorite holidays—just as if they still lived in their homeland. Many businesses and schools close on days that are religious holidays for only part of the population. The Jewish holiday, Yom Kippur, is just one example.

For most Canadians, Christmas and Easter are the two most important religious holidays of the year. Christmas in Canada is not the same for everyone, though. It is celebrated in different ways all across the country.

In small French-Canadian towns in Quebec, Christmas starts with Mass at midnight. French Canadians feast afterward, in the middle of the night. This feast is called *réveillon*. The meal includes frozen puddings, meat stews, and other old French dishes, such as *tourtiére*, which is a rich meat pie.

For these Canadian children, part of the fun of Christmas is window shopping for toys.

Canadians of Dutch origin have set up many communities all over eastern Canada. They have their own ideas about Christmas—and Santa Claus. For most children in the United States and Canada, Santa Claus travels around the world in a sleigh pulled by eight reindeer. But the Dutch believe that Santa Claus's sleigh is pulled by an eight-legged horse called Sleipner. Many Dutch Canadians start the Christmas season early, on December 5, St. Nicholas' Eve. Children fill their shoes with grain and put them out for Sleipner. If they have been good children, they will wake and find toys and presents. But if they have been bad, they wake up to find only sticks and twigs.

Ukrainian people who live in Canada celebrate their Christmas on January 6. That is the Epiphany—the day when the Christ child was first shown to the wise men. *Epiphany* is a Greek word that means "a showing." As the sun goes down on Christmas Eve, it is the children's job to watch for the first star to appear. Then it is time to eat. The family gathers around the dinner table for a twelve-course Christmas dinner. Each course has a special meaning in the Ukrainian culture.

At some point during this feast, the father will stand and offer a prayer. Afterward he will take a spoonful of *koot'yah*, boiled wheat and honey, and toss it in the air. In some families, the koot'yah is thrown at the ceiling. If the gooey mixture sticks to the ceiling, it means it will be a good year.

Christmas is also different for children who live in the far north of Canada. Inuit children have been known to say they want to see Santa Claus being pulled along by horses and cows instead of by reindeer. In the north, children see many deer and caribou, which look a lot like reindeer. But they hardly ever see horses or cows, so that would be a real treat for them.

Many native Indians learned of Christmas from the early British and French colonists and developed their own legends about Christmas. They believe that at midnight on Christmas Eve, all the deer in the forest kneel with their heads bowed toward Bethlehem—the town where Christ was born.

Easter celebrates Christ's rising from the dead. The date for Easter is not the same every year. It is the Sunday after the first full moon following March 21 (the first day of spring). The word *Easter* probably comes from an old English word, *eostre*. In some cultures, Eostre was the goddess of spring. On Easter, Christians in Canada go to church to remember Christ's resurrection. Easter is also a time for celebrating the beginning of spring.

As in much of the United States, dyed eggs, a symbol of new life, are made at this time. Before Easter many schoolchildren spend time in their art classes painting and dyeing eggs in bright colors and patterns. On Easter, children may search for colored eggs in an Easter-egg hunt.

Another favorite holiday of many Canadian boys and girls is St. Valentine's Day, which is celebrated on February 14. On this special date, people send valentines to those they like or love, just as they do in the United States.

Remembering History

Canada has important national holidays, too, such as Victoria Day, May 24. Victoria Day is the oldest national holiday in Canada. It marks the birthday of Queen

Victoria, who ruled the British Empire, including Canada, from 1837 to 1901.

Thanksgiving is also celebrated in Canada, but it is different from the holiday in the United States. It has not always been on the day it is now, the second Monday in October. Before Canada became a united country in 1867, each colony had its own Thanksgiving Day and gave thanks for different reasons. The first national Thanksgiving Day was declared in 1871 to show gratitude for the return to health of Britain's Prince of Wales. It has been celebrated all over Canada ever since.

Canadians celebrate their country's birthday on Canada Day, July 1, the date in 1867 when Canada officially became self-governing. Canadians mark the day with fireworks displays and parades.

Not all the special days in Canada are happy ones. Every year on November 11, Canadians mark Remembrance Day. At eleven o'clock in the morning, everybody is silent for two minutes to remember all the Canadian soldiers who died in the two World Wars.

People also buy "poppies," small red cloth or plastic flowers, and wear them on their shirts or coats. Poppies are special because they are found in Flanders Fields in Belgium, where many of the soldiers who died in World War I are buried.

Quebec's Celebrations

The holidays just described are some of the many special days that are marked by Canadians all over Canada. But not all holidays in Canada are celebrated by everybody. St. Jean Baptiste Day, for instance, is celebrated only in Quebec.

St. Jean Baptiste (in English, St. John the Baptist) is believed to be the person who baptized Christ, and every June 24 is devoted to him. That date is also close to the summer solstice, the longest day of the year. June 24 was chosen by French Canadians as their own special holiday to celebrate their French language and culture. They named the day after their patron saint. In 1977, St. Jean Baptiste Day became a legal holiday in Quebec.

St. Jean Baptiste Day was originally celebrated in Montreal and Quebec City with a big parade. People from all types of community organizations would march, wearing uniforms or costumes and displaying banners. In every parade there was always a float that carried a blond shepherd boy with curly hair and a pet lamb by his side. The lamb was always white with a bow around its neck. The boy represented St. Jean.

The parade in Montreal continues today, but the holiday is now celebrated all over the province of Quebec, too. The merrymaking usually begins at night. Musicians and singers come out to perform everybody's favorite

Celebrations take place all across Canada on Canada Day.

songs. As it gets dark, a huge bonfire is started in the middle of a big field. Over the years the celebration of St. Jean Baptiste Day has not changed very much, but in recent years the little shepherd boy who plays St. Jean Baptiste in the parade has been replaced by a young man.

Besides St. Jean Baptiste Day, Quebec City also celebrates a famous festival called Winter Carnival, which is held in the middle of winter, from February 6 to 16. Visitors come from all over the province to the ten-day celebration. There are two big parades during the carnival, and both are followed by all-night dancing. Another big attraction is the snow sculpture contest, which draws teams from all over the world. The fun at the carnival is always watched over by the *Bonhomme Carnival*—a giant snowman who smiles over everybody for all ten days of the celebration.

Regional Festivals

Other parts of Canada also have their own festivals. In Newfoundland it is a custom during the Christmas season to go mumming. The tradition of mumming first began with plays in Ireland and the United Kingdom in which actors wore disguises. In time this original form of mumming developed into the two different customs found in North America, the house visit and the parade.

*A snowman entertains visitors who have come to celebrate
Winter Carnival in Quebec City.*

Before going mumming, family members or friends
get together and disguise themselves. Dressing up so that
nobody will recognize you is the secret to being a good
mummer. Men sometimes dress up as women. Women
sometimes dress up as men. Or both may dress up as
sailors. Mummers may wear masks, veils, gloves, or even
paint that is safe for the skin. They change the way they
stand and walk. They also change the shape of their bodies
by putting pillows and pads inside their clothes.

Once the mummers feel they are fully disguised, they
go out into the neighborhood. When the group comes to a

This fair in Ontario features a log-sawing contest.

house, they knock on the door in a strange way. Then they call in a disguised voice, "Mummers allowed in?" Once the neighbors let them into the house, they dance around and tease their hosts. After a while the people take off their disguises and are served drinks by their host. When they are finished, they put their disguises on again and go out into the night to the next house. This festival lasts from December 25 to January 6. Many Newfoundlanders look forward to it all year.

The province of Ontario has many special holidays of its own. For nine days every summer, Toronto is the home of the International Caravan, a celebration of all the different peoples and cultures in Toronto and the rest of Canada. Greeks, Japanese, Ukrainians, and many other groups set up booths and offer their traditional foods, wines, and entertainment.

Canada's capital of Ottawa is a beautiful city all year round. But it is especially festive the last two weeks in May, during the Tulip Festival. During World War II, Canada provided a safe home for the royal family of the Netherlands. After the war, Queen Juliana of the Netherlands gave ten thousand tulip bulbs to Canada as a way of saying thank-you. The royal family still sends Ottawa these tulips every year.

The western provinces of Canada also host festivals. Boys and girls all over Canada know about the Calgary

Stampede. It is much like a huge rodeo, but there are many other events that make the Stampede special.

The Calgary Stampede runs for ten days in early July. Its most famous event is the chuck wagon race, in which small horse-drawn covered wagons compete against one another. There are also wild-cow milking contests, wild-horse races, and Indian buffalo riding. All the traditional rodeo contests are also featured. Before the Stampede starts, there is a big street parade with bands, floats, richly costumed Indians, and the best-dressed cowboys and cowgirls in Canada.

The western province of Alberta also holds the famous Klondike Days in Edmonton, which celebrate the gold rush. For ten days every July, Edmonton tries to recapture the spirit of that exciting time. One of the most popular events of Klondike Days is the "world championship sourdough raft race." The name sourdough is a reminder of the food eaten by prospectors in the north during the gold rush. (Klondike Days also feature breakfasts of pancakes made with sourdough.) People from Edmonton and all over Alberta come to this event with homemade boats made of bathtubs, wooden rafts, and anything else you can imagine. Some of the boats look so strange that it is difficult to tell they are boats.

In British Columbia, the land of vast forests, the lumberjack is the center of attention. Logging competitions are the highlight of festivals such as Canada Day in

*A Canadian cowboy struggles to stay in the saddle during a
rodeo event at the Calgary Stampede.*

Salmo, British Columbia. Logging events include log rolling, ax-throwing, and powersaw bucking.

All over the Northwest Territories and the Yukon, festivals are put on throughout the year by different Indian and Inuit tribes. There are many exciting events during these celebrations—dog races, dog-sled-pulling contests, and world-championship fiddling competitions. There are snowmobile races, beauty contests, parades, and bonfires, too.

One of the things people like the most at these festivals is the blanket-tossing event. A team of 100 people will hold a big blanket tightly so that it is like a trampoline. One person is on the stretched blanket. Each team wins points for keeping the person on the blanket bouncing in the air the longest. The jumper also wins points for putting on an interesting show.

The names of some of the festivals in the Territories and the Yukon are just as interesting as the events—Toonik Tyme in Frobisher Bay, the Ookpik Carnival in Hay River, and the Wood Buffalo Frolics at Fort Smith. These festivals in the far north feature traditional Inuit activities such as dancing and sports. But they also include competitions that test survival skills in the freezing cold, such as animal-skinning.

Whatever the season, the day, the occasion, or the people, Canadians use their festivals to show how much they have to celebrate.

LIVING—AND EATING—IN CANADA

Whenever they can, many Canadian families try to make holiday plans that include spending time in the Canadian countryside, where they can enjoy the crisp air and breathtaking wilderness that make them so proud of their country. Many families own small cabins in the countryside, which they visit on weekends or during their holidays. Some lie deep in the woods. Others are located along the shores of Canada's countless lakes.

Cabin owners try to spend as much of their summer as possible at their cabins. There is much to keep them and their families busy. Those with lakeshore cabins can use the lake for water sports. Adults and children alike enjoy windsurfing and sailing. When they feel like relaxing, they can blow up their air mattresses, float around, and soak up the sun.

When night begins to fall, families often light the barbecue. Friends and neighbors from nearby cabins may be invited over after dinner to roast marshmallows over the glowing embers of the fire. The activity and fresh air can be tiring, though and by late evening, everyone is ready for bed. They often fall asleep listening to crickets chirp a peaceful song.

But not every family owns a cabin. Others would rather travel and see other parts of Canada on their holidays. For example, many Canadians, as well as United States tourists, visit Niagara Falls each year. These spectacular falls, on the United States-Canadian border, actually consist of two waterfalls. The American Falls are on the U.S. side of the border in New York. The Horseshoe Falls are on the Canadian side in Ontario.

Many Canadian families visit the public beaches on Canada's bigger lakes. Other beach lovers flock to the Maritime Provinces of New Brunswick and Nova Scotia, which have long sandy beaches on the Atlantic. On Prince Edward Island, the beaches are made of a coarse, rusty-red sand on the south shore and a fine white sand on the north shore. It, too, is a favorite vacation place.

Other families prefer the woods and mountains to the water and like to spend their vacations in the many small towns nestled among Canada's Rocky Mountains. They often enjoy hiking in the woods and climbing some of the smaller mountains.

The coast of British Columbia seems to have something for every kind of visitor. There are rivers and inland lakes for water sports. There are beautiful beaches, as there are on the East Coast. And there are majestic mountains and vast forests. Many Canadians visit British Columbia for the salmon fishing. The powerful salmon are

Tourists enjoy the spectacular view of Niagara Falls.

not easy to catch, but the reward is well worth the effort. Salmon is a delicious fish.

Canada is also a country of enthusiastic campers. The government has worked to preserve Canada's natural beauty and wildlife. Across Canada huge areas of land have been set aside as national and provincial parks. All together, Canada's parks cover 150,000 square miles.

Canadian Lifestyles

In many ways, Canadians across the country lead very different lives. In fact, it is very difficult to describe a typical Canadian family, since a family living in the Montreal suburb of Pointe Claire may lead a very different life from a farm family near the small town of Jenner, Alberta, and a family in Fort Franklin, in the Northwest Territories, may have a different way of life from someone in the provinces to the south.

Tim and Jean Gabriel, for instance, have lived in Pointe Claire all their lives. Their parents moved to Canada from the West Indies as a young couple, and through hard work they established themselves in the community. Tim and Jean's father is a music teacher at a nearby public high school. Their mother has her own practice as a family doctor.

The Gabriels are a busy family, with many interests and hobbies. They are also a two-language family. They usually speak English at home, but they also set aside times when they speak only French. They all realize how important it is to be bilingual in Quebec, and what a good skill it would be to have if they ever move to another province.

During the school year fifteen-year-old Jean spends a lot of time in downtown Montreal, where she must travel every day by bus to go to her school. She does not like all the traveling, but her dream is to be a ballerina, and the place where she studies ballet is in the city. Some days she does not get home from her classes until late at night. Her parents sometimes wish they could see her more, but they know it takes a lot of time and practice to become a ballerina. They remember how proud they were when their daughter won a spot in the ballet *The Nutcracker Suite*. When school is out, Jean spends a lot of time at home with her friends and at the local pool, where she is training to be a lifeguard.

Her younger brother, Tim, also keeps a busy schedule. His parents encourage his love of sports, but they sometimes wish his morning hockey practices did not start at six o'clock. In the winter it is pitch black when Tim must be driven to the arena. He is also interested in music and has saved enough money from his afternoon paper route to buy a bass guitar and an amplifier. His parents let him use a small room in the basement to practice.

Weekdays are busy in the Gabriel household, and opportunities to spend time together are rare. But on the weekend the family often sets out on one of their favorite day trips. In the winter they might go to a nearby golf club, which is open to the public for cross-country skiing. And in summer they like to ride their bikes along the bike paths near the St. Lawrence River.

Other Canadian families are not always able to relax in the summer. The Richardson family of Jenner, Alberta, owns a wheat farm that has been passed down through three generations. Living there are four teenage girls, an eleven-year-old boy, their parents, and their father's parents, who have lived on the farm since they were a young couple. The children love animals. In the barn they keep a horse and the boy's pet pig—the runt of the litter, given to him by a neighbor. There are also two dogs and a cat.

Like the Gabriels, the Richardsons lead a busy life. But their busy schedule is different. The farm is the focus of their attention, especially in summer. From spring until fall the wheat fields must be constantly tended and the machinery kept in good working order. As in all farm families, everyone has chores to do. Even the grandparents pitch in.

With all the hard work, mealtimes are important for the Richardson family. Breakfast is served early in the morning, and it has to provide enough energy to keep

Chores are a fact of life for everyone living on a farm.

everyone going until lunch. Eggs, pancakes, or hot cereal are often served at breakfast. The Richardsons generally have their big meal of the day at around five o'clock. By that time, everyone is usually hungry and eager for a good, hearty meal.

After cleaning up the dinner dishes, the Richardson family has a chance to relax. Sometimes they read or watch television. Once a week the girls are driven into town for their 4-H Club meeting, where they learn about everything from sewing to photography. Since most farm families live by similar schedules, Boy Scout meetings are usually held the same night as the 4-H Club so parents do not have to make too many trips into town during the week. Since the family's day starts early the next morning, the meetings usually end by nine o'clock.

Soon after the wheat is harvested, the fields are blanketed with a layer of snow. But the children's chores do not end with the summer farming. They take turns using the tractor to clear snow from their long driveway before they go off to school, and the animals must be cared for and protected against the often bitter cold of winter.

The cold temperatures the Richardsons are familiar with do not come close to the cold experienced by Inuit families living in Fort Franklin, in the Northwest Territories. Fort Franklin is a small town about 400 miles north of Yellowknife. The community is like many others

A tepee-shaped church in Fort Franklin reminds visitors of the many native people living in the Canadian territories.

in the Canadian north. The families live between two cultures, keeping many of their own traditions and customs but also being influenced by many aspects of present-day Canadian society.

Inuit homes are up-to-date. They have refrigerators and stoves and televisions. With satellite dishes, some of the families are able to receive Canadian and American television shows. In school the children are taught many of the same subjects as other Canadian children to the south. But ties to Inuit culture are strong. The Inuit still hunt, trap, and fish the way their ancestors did generations ago.

The lifestyles of families in different regions of Canada vary widely. Their schedules are not the same because their lives revolve around different kinds of work and play. Canada's immense size explains these differences. Canada's geography and climate change dramatically from coast to coast and from north to south, affecting the way Canadians live and work. But most Canadians are united by the love of their country and their interest in the many different cultures within Canada's borders.

Canadian Cooking

The great diversity of the Canadian people is also reflected in the different foods that are found across the country. The Maritime Provinces, for example, are famous for their seafood—best when eaten fresh. Families vacationing in Prince Edward Island are especially fond of clambakes on the beach. The first thing needed for a clambake is a big pot of water boiling over a bonfire on the beach. The clams are dug up, rinsed, then dropped in the pot to cook. When the clams are done, everybody finds a warm spot on the sand to enjoy their fresh-from-the-sea dinner.

Prince Edward Island also has many strawberry farms where families can go to pick their own berries. Pick-your-own farms offer an inexpensive way to get fresh fruit. You can also choose the strawberries you think are the best. The fresh berries are wonderful in pies and with ice cream.

New Brunswick is the home of an interesting vegetable. Its real name is the ostrich fern sprout, but most people call it the fiddlehead. When these ferns first start to grow in the early spring, their tops are curled so tightly that they look like the heads of violins or fiddles. Fiddleheads are best when they are fried with fresh fish and butter.

If fiddleheads sound strange to you, then you may not have heard of edible seaweed either. Also found in New Brunswick, this seaweed is called dulse. People gather it at low tide in the Bay of Fundy. But they do not eat it right away. Dulse is first dried in the sun, which causes it to turn purple. It is then eaten raw or added to casseroles and chowders. Dulse has a rubbery texture and tastes odd the first time you eat it. Even so, it is popular. An added bonus is that it contains a lot of iodine, which means it's very good for you.

A little farther west, in Quebec, foods are somewhat richer. One of the oldest traditional foods is the *tourtiére*—the rich meat pie made with gravy, pastry, and ground meat. Another hearty dish is a stew made of meatballs and pigs' feet, whose French name is *ragoût de boulettes et de pattes de cochon*. The dish is made with real pigs' feet (or pigs' knuckles, as they are also called). Many people say that when it is cooked properly, the meat around the bones of the pig's feet is delicious. Other traditional dishes include pea soup and French onion soup, which are hailed for their ability to warm and fill an empty stomach on a cold winter's day.

Montreal is also famous for a dish called *poutine*, which is made with French fries, cheese, and gravy. To make it, you fill a bowl with hot cooked French fries and then sprinkle lumps of white cheddar cheese on top. Over these you pour a slightly spicy, hot gravy and then wait for the gravy to melt the cheese.

In the early spring, when the sap is starting to run in the maple trees, families often travel to spend the day at one of Quebec's many sugar shacks. The shacks are usually located deep in the woods.

Sugar shacks, like this one in the woods of eastern Canada, produce a variety of maple syrup products.

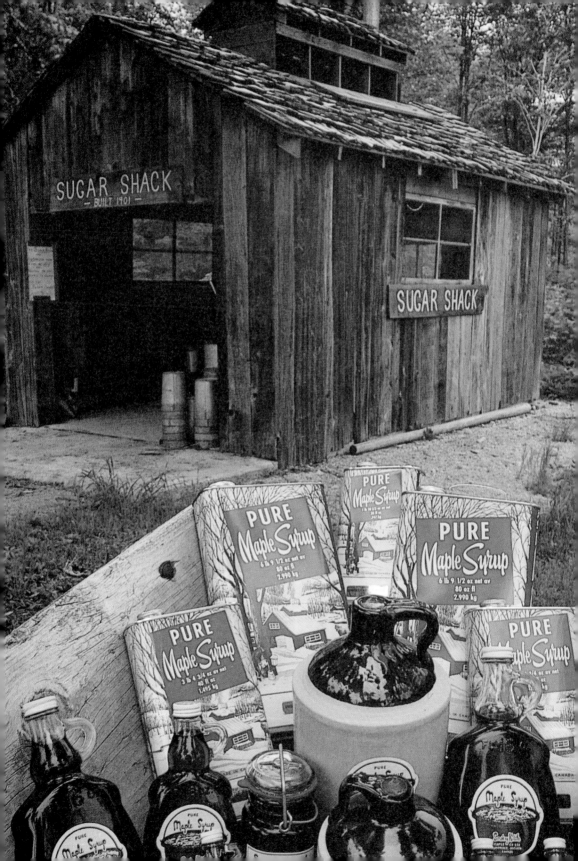

At a "sugaring off," maple-syrup producers sell
samples of maple-syrup products. You have to come
prepared for a full day of eating. The sweet sap that is
drawn out of the trees is boiled into syrup and used in
several dishes put out for the hungry guests. There are eggs
cooked in boiling maple syrup, ham cooked in maple
syrup, and candies, breads, pies, cookies, and cakes,
all made with maple syrup. These food ideas were
borrowed from the Indian tribes, who originally tapped the
sweet liquid and cooked it with almost anything you can
imagine. A favorite part of the sugaring off for many
children is the making of *tourquettes*. Boiling maple syrup
is poured from the vats onto a fresh patch of clean snow.
The sap begins to harden right away, and freshly cut sticks
from trees are used to turn and mold this natural candy.

Ontario is known for its excellent farmland, which
produces many kinds of food. Its orchards and farms
supply a wide variety of fruits and vegetables that brigh-
ten the markets in Ontario's big cities throughout the summer. It is also world-famous for its cheeses, such as cheddar. Roast pheasant and pumpkin pie are just two special
dishes that Ontario cooks prepare.

Farther west, in the Prairie Provinces of Manitoba,
Saskatchewan, and Alberta, many families have a tradition
of big, hearty meals. Winters on the prairies can be cold
and long, and time passes more easily when it is spent with

fine food and good friends. Parts of the western provinces have become famous for their sausage and smoked meat and fish. Smoked food stays fresh longer.

If you ask Canadians what food British Columbia is best known for, they are sure to say salmon. People come from around the world to try to catch this big fish as it swims upstream from the ocean to reach its spawning grounds.

British Columbia is also well known for a few other foods. The Okanagan Valley, which lies inland, is known all over Canada as a place to get crisp vegetables and fruit, especially apples and peaches. And British Columbians are also famous for their love of chocolate. A delicious chocolate bar is made at a place in British Columbia called Nanaimo. A Nanaimo Bar is best described as a layered chocolate cookie bar, and it is legendary among chocolate lovers in Canada. The best way to understand the popularity of Nanaimo Bars is to try one yourself. The recipe is a bit complicated, so you might need to ask an experienced cook to help you.

Nanaimo Bars
(British Columbia)

Bottom layer
1/2 cup butter
1/4 cup granulated sugar

1/3 cup unsweetened cocoa

1 teaspoon vanilla

1 egg, beaten

1 cup unsweetened dried coconut

2 cups graham wafer (cracker) crumbs

1/2 cup chopped walnuts

Filling

1/4 cup butter (1/2 stick)

2 tablespoons milk

2 tablespoons instant vanilla custard or vanilla pudding powder

2 cups sifted powdered (icing) sugar

Topping

4 oz. unsweetened baking chocolate

1 tablespoon butter

1. To make the bottom layer: Melt the butter in a saucepan over low heat. Add the sugar, cocoa, vanilla, and egg. Cook, stirring over medium heat, until the mixture thickens. Remove from heat and stir in the coconut, cracker crumbs, and walnuts. Pat firmly into a buttered nine-inch square baking pan. Refrigerate for at least one hour.

2. To make the filling: Cream the butter with a hand mixer. Beat in the milk, custard powder, and powdered sugar. If the mixture is too thick to spread, add a few more drops of milk. Spread over the bottom

layer and refrigerate for 30 minutes, or until firm.

3. For the top layer: Melt the chocolate and butter in a dish set over hot water. Spread over the filling and refrigerate. Before the chocolate hardens completely, cut into squares. Refrigerate for at least one hour. Then enjoy!

As you can imagine, the meals are big and hearty in the Yukon and the Northwest Territories. Good food is a must for energy and warmth most of the year. To get the day off to a good start, the breakfasts served in the north are huge. They often include pancakes, chicken, bacon, sausage, and eggs.

A lot of the meats eaten in the north are not kinds most of us are used to. The most popular meat in the Yukon is moose. In the Territories the favorite meat is caribou. Many of the people hunt for the meat themselves. Cattle cannot survive in the harsh cold, and so the Inuit often eat bear or even muskox. A lot of people who come to the north do not like the thought of eating these animals. To make them more appealing, meats like roast muskox are called polar beef instead.

The fish of the north is delicious. Many people believe that the freezing cold waters make northern fish meat richer and tastier. If you ever get the chance, try Arctic Char and find out for yourself.

Arctic Char
(Ontario)

3 to 4 pounds of Arctic char fillets (or other meaty
   white fish)
1 cup oil
1/4 cup vinegar
1/2 teaspoon garlic powder
1 teaspoon thyme

1. Mix together the oil, vinegar, and spices. Pour the
   mixture over the fish fillets, and allow to stand (in
   the refrigerator) for 2 to 4 hours.
2. When ready to cook, drain the fish. Place it on a
   broiler pan and brush with a little more oil. Broil
   it about 5 inches from the broiler heat. Allow 10
   minutes cooking time for every one-inch thickness
   of the fillets, and turn the fillets over halfway
   through cooking. The fish will be done when
   it comes apart easily (flakes) when probed
   with a fork.

You might wish to accompany your fish with fresh,
sliced British Columbia tomatoes (sprinkle each slice with
a little dried dill weed or powdered thyme) and wild rice,
a Manitoba specialty.

Wild Rice
(Manitoba)

1 cup wild rice
4 cups water
1/2 pound fresh mushrooms, sliced
2 sprigs celery leaves, chopped
1/2 green pepper, diced
1 medium onion, chopped
1 tablespoon chopped parsley
1 tablespoon pimento
1 tablespoon butter
1/2 teaspoon Italian seasoning
Pinch of thyme
Salt and pepper
1/2 cup chicken broth

1. In a large sieve or colander, wash the wild rice. Put the rice and the water into a large saucepan. Bring to a boil, then simmer the rice for one hour. Drain.
2. In the butter, cook the mushrooms, celery leaves, green pepper, onion, parsley, and pimento until the onion is soft. Add the Italian seasoning, thyme, and broth to the vegetables. Add salt and pepper to taste.
3. Mix the rice and the cooked vegetables together, and heat together until piping hot.

This wild rice dish tastes even better the day after it is made!

Akutaq is another dish sometimes eaten by families in certain parts of the north. Akutaq is a combination of boiled fish, berries, and sugar with shortening and oil (seal oil, if it's available!). The mixture is frozen and forms a kind of ice cream. The extreme cold of winters in the north calls for food that is satisfying and energy producing. The large amount of fat in this mixture makes akutaq just such a food.

The bounty of food from Canadian farms reaches across the country.

8

VARIED EDUCATIONS

Canadian and American children have many things in common, and school is one of them. School plays a big part in children's lives in Canada, just as it does in the United States. School is a place to learn. Children also think of school as a place to meet friends. Although American and Canadian schools are somewhat alike, Canadian schools are also special in their own ways.

In most provinces and territories, elementary school goes to grade six. Then comes two years of junior high school, and finally, high school from grades nine to twelve. But children in Quebec go straight from elementary school to high school—which goes only to grade eleven. Ontario has the same system as most other provinces, except that high school goes to grade thirteen.

People are often surprised to learn that students in different parts of Canada graduate from high school at different ages. When Canada became a nation in 1867, it was agreed that decisions about education would be made by each province. Each province sets up its school system to suit itself.

Religion also plays a part in many Canadian schools. In Quebec, for example, the French and English-language schools are run as Protestant or Catholic schools. But in other provinces the schools are not all organized around religions. Most are funded by the government, although as in Quebec, some schools are run by the Roman Catholic Church. Canada is a land of great variety, and as you can see, the school systems are no exception.

The School Day

Most Canadian students begin their day around eight or nine in the morning. Their first class is usually their home class. The teacher takes attendance and lets students know about any important events that will take place that week.

Like American students, Canadians take classes in a wide variety of subjects. There are courses that every student takes, such as math, Canadian history, geography, biology, chemistry, physics, and literature. Since French and English are Canada's two official languages, every Canadian is taught how to speak a second language.

These courses are the serious areas of study. But there are other classes in which students can have fun while learning some practical skills. Students can learn how to cook in home economics class or how to change car tires in auto shop. There are also woodworking classes, in which students may make handmade cutting boards, for example. In metal shop many students build toolboxes. Music and art classes are also very popular.

*The kinds of schools that Canadian children attend vary
from province to province, because when Canada became a nation,
provincial governments were given the right to set up
their school systems.*

Games and Fun

If you asked Canadian students about their favorite part of the school day, they would probably say, "Recess!" During recess, students can work off all their extra energy. Sometimes small groups play their own games in the schoolyard. At other times, everybody joins in for one big game.

"British Bulldog" is a game that everybody can play. All the players stand at one end of a field, with one person in the middle who is "it." When he or she yells "British Bulldog!" everyone tries to run to the other side without being caught. If a player is caught, he or she joins the players in the middle. When they yell "British Bulldog" again, the people in the middle help catch more people. The winner is the last person to be caught.

Perhaps the most popular schoolyard game is hockey. In winter a part of the schoolyard is usually made into a small skating rink. Students bring their skates and hockey sticks in the morning and play whenever they get a break from classes. The hockey does not stop in the spring and fall, either. It is still played in the schoolyard, usually in running shoes.

When school is out, some students stay after school for more British Bulldog or hockey before it is time to go home. Others stay for special clubs where they can talk about their hobbies or special interests. Students can join photography, music, chess, and astronomy clubs, for example.

Organized sports are also offered by Canadian schools. One day out of every year is set aside as Track and Field Day. Students get a break from their studies to compete with their classmates. But the competition is not always serious. There are many laughs, especially when the teachers join in the fun.

For students who really like sports, schools usually have organized teams and leagues. All kinds of sports are played in these leagues—football, basketball, soccer, volleyball, and swimming are just a few examples. In elementary schools the teams are usually organized for intramurals, in which students play only against other students in their own school. These teams are organized in leagues that compete when classes end for the day. In high school the teams compete against other schools' teams. Sometimes the whole school turns out to cheer.

Organized trips are also a big part of school life. Schools often arrange exchange trips with schools in different parts of their province. In Quebec, French-language schools run exchange programs with English-language schools. This way, everybody can learn about a culture other than their own. Classes are also often taken to see plays or to visit one of Canada's famous museums. Teachers in Canada believe it is important for students to be exposed to as much Canadian culture as possible.

Crafts such as pottery making are often taught in art classes.

Both trips and special programs brought to schools are considered important to students' education. These children are participating in a program called Jungles Alive.

Schools in the North

Not every school in Canada is near a museum or theater. In fact, some Canadian schools are very far from big cities. Many Inuit children, for example, live hundreds of miles from a city. Their school life is much different from what most students know.

Some Inuit communities still hunt for much of their food. And the school year must follow the hunting season. At some point each winter, the older boys are taken out of school to learn about surviving in the wilderness. They are taught how to make igloos—a skill that could save their lives in a sudden Arctic storm. They also learn how to make sleds, how to tell direction from the way the wind blows, and how to tell what lies over the horizon by reading the reflections on the clouds.

School life in the far north is different in other ways, too. Television plays an important role in northern communities. It is a link with the rest of Canada. Many children in the north watch a lot of TV. Because the students see things that are new to them on television, the teacher often discusses shows in class the next day.

Once in a while, recess at the northern schools has to be cut short, or even canceled—because of polar bears. The powerful white animals often stray into northern towns looking for food. Children must stay indoors for their own safety until the bears are persuaded to leave.

Before the 1970s native Canadian children were often bussed to nearby schools operated by the provincial governments. If they were too far from these public schools, they were sent to boarding schools, where they would learn the same subjects as all other Canadian children. But in 1972 the national government adopted a new policy that allowed native Canadian children to be taught by native Canadian teachers. Children could learn about their native language and the traditional values of their culture. The government helped build hundreds of schools so that these children would no longer have to be bussed to provincial schools or sent away to boarding school.

After High School

Canadian high-school students have to think about what they will do after they graduate—whether they will get a job or attend a university. Students can also enroll in community colleges, where they can receive a certificate or diploma in a commercial field, such as advertising. There are also technical schools, where students can learn such subjects as electronics.

Earning a degree, certificate, or diploma takes dedication. College courses are not easy. Students must work long hours. There is a lot of competition, since most Canadian students are hard workers who want high marks.

University students have to work hard to graduate. The Canadian government helps students to attend a university by paying most of the costs of a university education.

Going to a university can cost a lot of money. Canadian leaders have always believed that students who are bright and eager should be able to get the schooling they want. They decided that the government would pay for most of the cost of going to a university so that even those who could not afford such an education on their own could get the education they wanted. The government also grants large loans to students.

There are 70 universities in Canada, and some are among the best in the world. Students from as far away as Japan travel to Canada for a top-notch education. The biggest university in Canada is also one of its best— the University of Toronto. In fact, many Americans refer to the University of Toronto as the Harvard of the North, after the famous university in Massachusetts. Some Canadians think the comparison should be the other way around. They wear sweatshirts that say, "Harvard—the U of T of the South!"

Canada's educational system is admired around the world. In their elementary and high-school years, students are taught by well-trained teachers in both French and English. There are also well-developed athletic programs and extracurricular programs for students with hobbies. And once they have graduated from high school, students enjoy the freedom to choose whatever path they wish, thanks to the government's support of higher education.

LOVE OF SPORT

Almost all Canadians love the outdoors and find many ways to enjoy themselves in it. Canadian boys and girls share many favorite games with Americans, such as basketball and baseball. Children also like to get together for games of softball, volleyball, or touch football. Sports such as skating and hockey are especially popular in Canada. Many Canadian children skate or play hockey every chance they get, whether on homemade skating rinks or in organized leagues. Lack of ice does not stop them—in summer, they play street hockey.

In addition to playing sports for fun, Canadians believe it is important to learn to play in organized leagues and teams. Playing on a team helps children learn to be good sports, to lead others, and to work with others. The Sport Canada department in the national government works to make sure there is a sport and team for every eager boy and girl.

Basketball and Lacrosse

Several sports played around the world owe their start to Canadians. People are often surprised to learn that basketball was invented by a Canadian. Born in Ontario,

James Naismith played an early version of basketball as a young boy with his friends. They aimed large balls at open-bottomed peach baskets that were nailed to posts. Naismith later moved to Springfield, Massachusetts, and became an instructor at the local YMCA. He introduced his childhood game when the boys he was teaching complained they were bored. The first official game of basketball was played on January 20, 1892.

Canadians also began the game of lacrosse, which is now played in England, the United States, Australia, and New Zealand. The game was invented by Canadian Plains Indians, who called their game *baggatway*. French missionaries changed the name to *lacrosse* because the webbed stick used in the game looked to them like a bishop's "shepherd's crook"—*crosse* in French.

Men's lacrosse is a very fast game. Players on ten-man teams use sticks with a net pocket at the end to catch, throw, or carry a small rubber ball to score goals in their opponent's net (which looks somewhat like a small soccer goal). Only the goalkeeper may touch the ball with his hands; the other players must use their sticks or feet to move the ball. Women's lacrosse is much like men's, but the game is less rough and slightly shorter and is played with twelve team members.

When Canada became self-governing in 1867, one of the government's first acts was to declare lacrosse the official game of Canada. It has been popular throughout Canada's history. Teams compete for trophies such as the Mann Cup, first presented in 1910.

Canadian Hockey

Many people think that ice hockey, not lacrosse, is Canada's true national sport. It too was invented in Canada, but people disagree about where it was first played. Some say that soldiers played the first game in the 1850s as a type of field hockey. The rules were written by students at McGill University in Montreal. Even the puck was invented at McGill. A student thought that a flat disk would work better than the rubber ball originally used, so he sliced a one-inch-thick section out of the ball and created the first hockey puck.

Just as hockey was born in Canada, it seems Canadians were born to play hockey. Many stars of professional hockey have come out of Canada, among them Maurice Richard, Gordie Howe, Bobby Hull, Guy Lapointe, Bobby Orr, Phil and Tony Esposito, and Jacques Plante. But the player whom many consider the greatest hockey player of all time is Wayne Gretzky.

Almost as soon as he could walk, Wayne was whizzing around the floor of his living room with his toy hockey stick and ball, imitating the players he saw on *Hockey*

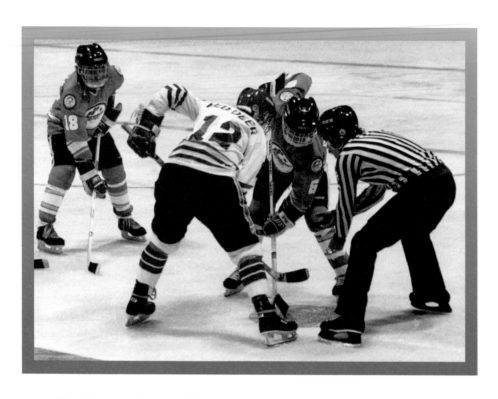

The fast-paced game of hockey is a Canadian favorite. Many of the best hockey players in the world come from Canada.

Night in Canada, the TV broadcast of games. He joined his first league when he was only five and scored just one goal that season. But when he was eleven, Wayne scored 378 goals in one season! Wayne was already a budding superstar. At an early age, he learned to give interviews for TV and radio. Fans asked him for autographs. Sometimes, people would even steal his stick or gloves as souvenirs.

When he began to play hockey professionally, Wayne Gretzky broke almost every National Hockey League scoring record. He signed contracts with hockey teams for millions of dollars. It is natural to think that such success must have changed Wayne. But it didn't seem to. He gave freely of his time to charity events and is still thoughtful, patient, and modest. "I'm just a country Canadian," Wayne says about himself. His success, and the success of so many Canadian players, encourages children to dream of and practice for a career in hockey.

Winter and Summer Sports

Another popular winter sport in Canada is skiing. People come from all over the world to ski in the Rocky Mountains of Alberta and British Columbia. Some of the mountains are so tall that the only way to get to their tops is by helicopter. Once there the lucky skiers cut through the powdery, pristine snow.

Children in all parts of Canada also like to go sledding, called tobogganing in Canada. Sometimes they bring their sleds to school and go tobogganing on a nearby hill at recess. Most children do not care if they have no sled. They use inner tubes from tires or big pieces of cardboard, or sometimes they just slide down on their backsides!

Canada is a good place for summer sports, too. Baseball, softball, bicycling, and soccer are enjoyed by Canadians of all ages. There are also many community pools for cooling off on a hot day.

Professional Sports and the Olympics

Young fans of professional sports can follow and cheer for Canadian baseball, football, and basketball teams. Canada's two baseball teams are the Toronto Blue Jays, of the American League, and the Montreal Expos, of the National League. For football fans there is the Canadian Football League, with five teams in western Canada and four in the east. Many teams have names that reflect Canada's heritage, such as the Calgary Stampeders and the Edmonton Eskimos. There are also two Canadian teams in the National Basketball Association—the Toronto Raptors and the Vancouver Grizzlies. Most of the baseball and football players on Canadian teams are American. But this is more than made up for by all the Canadians who play on American hockey teams.

Canadians also enjoy watching their athletes compete in the Olympics. At the 1984 Summer Olympics, in Los Angeles, California, Canadian athletes won the most medals ever for Canada: 10 gold, 18 silver, and 16 bronze. Canada finished fourth overall in the medal standings.

Many of the medals were won by Canadian swimmers. Anne Ottenbrite and Victor Davis both won several medals. But the swimmer who seemed to capture the hearts of all Canadians was twenty-year-old Alex Baumann. Tall and slender, Alex sped through the water to win two gold medals and one silver for Canada. The first Canadian to

A skier plunges down a snowy slope in the Canadian Rockies.

win two gold Olympic swimming medals since 1912, Baumann was a national hero when he returned to his hometown of Sudbury, Ontario. The town had a parade in his honor—even the prime minister was in the crowd. After the parade a car dealer gave him the keys to the sporty red convertible he was riding in. A local park was even named after him.

Canadians have excelled in more recent Olympics as well. One of the heroes of the 1992 Summer Olympics was Silken Laumann. She won the bronze medal in rowing for Canada, although she had to compete in tremendous pain. Only two months before the Olympics, her right leg was injured when her boat collided with another that crossed its path. Her leg required five operations, and doctors warned that she might never compete again. But she continued to train and inspired Canadians with her success. After winning her medal, Silken said, "I never stopped believing it was possible."

Canada has produced many other great athletes, including Steve Podborski, the first North American male skier to win a World Cup championship, and Lionel Conacher, an amazing all-around athlete who wrestled, boxed, and played championship lacrosse, baseball, professional hockey, and professional football. Whether they compete professionally or in the Olympics, play in leagues or with friends, or just enjoy watching others play, Canadians are true sports lovers.

Damon Stoudamire of the Toronto Raptors

THE FRIENDLY BORDER

Many brothers and sisters fight when they are young but become good friends as adults. In the same way, Canada and the United States have fought and struggled as they have grown into strong and independent nations. Today, Canada and the United States share a friendship unlike that of any other countries in the world.

Most Canadians feel that the United States is their country's best friend. A close look at the border between the two countries shows this to be true. In some places the border passes right through the middle of towns that are American on one side and Canadian on the other. Sometimes the border goes right through the middle of houses. The border that separates the two countries is unlike any other border in the world. When you realize that about 70 million people cross between the countries every year, the border seems to disappear. Seventy million is almost three times the population of Canada.

Americans in Canada

For many reasons, thousands of Americans have come to Canada to make new homes. When oil was discovered in Alberta, for example, oil-rig workers from Texas and

Every year millions of Americans travel to Canada for special events such as this fisheries festival in New Brunswick.

Oklahoma came to Canada for jobs. Just like other immigrants, Americans are made to feel right at home. In Ontario one group of people from the United States has formed the "American Club of Toronto."

Many Americans have made Canada their second home since the early days of Canadian history. As many as 3 million Americans may have settled in Canada since the 1700s. The rate at which Americans have moved to Canada has generally been quite steady. But there have been times when Americans have poured over the border into Canada.

Perhaps the greatest wave of Americans entered Canada between 1775 and 1784, during and after the American Revolution. The 13 British colonies in what is now the United States were fighting for their independence from Britain. But some colonists supported Britain during the Revolution. Because of their loyalty to the British Crown, they were called Loyalists. Considered the enemy by the colonists fighting in the Revolution, many Loyalists moved to Canada. Following the surrender of the British, between 40,000 and 50,000 Loyalists moved to Ontario, Quebec, and the Atlantic Provinces.

Thousands of African Americans also moved to Canada. They left the United States to escape slavery. African Americans moved to Canada over a period of about 100 years—from 1763 to 1865, when slaves in the United States were finally freed.

In the early 1900s the railways began to open up the West in Canada. At the same time, farmers in the United States were having trouble finding cheap farmland. Thousands of American farmers packed up their homes and families to accept the Canadian government's offer of land and new opportunities. They poured into Canada by the trainload.

The most recent American emigration to Canada happened during the 1960s and 1970s, when many Americans fled to Canada to avoid the draft during the Vietnam War. Other Americans moved from the United States to Canada because they were opposed to the war.

Canadians in the United States

Canadians have also moved to the United States by the thousands. Every year about 16,000 Canadians make new homes in the United States. Since 1820 more than 4 million Canadians have moved to the United States. Some bring their Canadian heritage with them and try to keep it alive.

Probably the first Canadians in the United States were the Acadians. In 1713, France surrendered Acadia to Britain. When many Acadians refused to live under British rule, thousands were moved to New Orleans. A part of that city is still called the French Quarter. In addition, many French Canadians live in Los Angeles. Every June 24 they celebrate St. Jean Baptiste Day, just as if they were at home in Quebec. Many French Canadians have also made their homes in the northeastern states of New Hampshire, Vermont, and Maine. As far south as Connecticut, some towns are home to so many French Canadians that many children grow up with French as their first language.

Florida is another popular spot for Canadians to settle. Thousands of French- and English-speaking Canadians have found new homes in the Sunshine State. And every winter, thousands more Canadians visit the warm Florida beaches to get away from the snow and cold.

Canadian Contributions

Canadians have made many contributions to life in the United States. Even before the United States was a nation, explorers and settlers from French Canada traveled into the unsettled wilderness to the south and left their mark in the names of places now in the United States, such as Baton Rouge, Terre Haute, Des Moines, and the Belle Fourche River in South Dakota and Wyoming. For the people who live in or near such places, the names are a constant reminder of their friendly neighbor to the north.

Other aspects of life in the United States also represent Canadian contributions. If you live in California and want to talk to someone in New York, all you have to do is pick up the phone. The person you can thank for this luxury was a Canadian—Alexander Graham Bell. Bell was born in Scotland in 1847 but became a Canadian when he moved to Brantford, Ontario, at the age of twenty-three. He invented the telephone a few years later and founded the Bell Telephone Company in 1876.

Communication by telephone has changed quite a bit since the days of Alexander Graham Bell. Many telephone lines have been replaced by satellite systems, which were put in space by the U.S. space shuttles. The satellites were taken up in the cargo bays of the shuttles and then released in orbit. When the satellites broke down, astronauts fixed them. They launched new satellites and recovered damaged satellites with the help of a long robot arm called the Canadarm. As its name shows, a team of Canadian scientists invented this useful device.

The lives of countless Americans, and of people all over the world, have been saved by the contribution of two Canadians to the world of medicine. Drs. Frederick Banting and Charles Best invented insulin, which is used the world over for the treatment of diabetes. People who have diabetes are not able to use the sugar they eat, and so the sugar stays in their blood. Insulin helps their bodies get rid of this sugar, which otherwise could cause death.

In most northern states in the United States, snow mobiles are a common sight and sound in the winter. Some

The robot arm used on space shuttle missions for releasing and retrieving space satellites was invented in Canada.

families use them to have fun, but many people use them for work—for instance, farmers use snowmobiles to cross snowy fields. The first snowmobile, or Ski-Doo®, was built in 1937 by a Quebecer named J. Armand Bombardier. The snowmobile is also important to Canadians, especially the Inuit. For them it is just like a car—they use it to go everywhere.

Have you ever played Trivial Pursuit®? This game, which took North America by storm in the mid-1980s, was invented by two Canadian journalists, Chris Haney and Scott Abbott. They thought up the game in a kitchen in Montreal, and it has since made them millionaires.

These are just a few examples of how Canadians have made life both easier and more fun.

Famous Canadian Americans

There are also many examples of Canadians who moved to the United States, developed successful careers, and became well known throughout the world. Cyrus Eaton was a Canadian who became a successful business owner in the United States in the early 1900s, where he founded the Republic Steel Company. Though he spent most of his life in the United States, he became best known for the Pugwash Conferences, held in his hometown of Pugwash, Nova Scotia. These meetings bring together scientists and world leaders to work for peace and other important issues. Eaton received the Lenin Peace Prize in 1960 for his efforts.

Another famous Canadian American who was successful in business was Samuel Bronfman. Born in Manitoba in 1891, he began his career delivering wood to houses. He moved into the hotel business and eventually became involved in the liquor business, especially in the United States. His financial empire grew, and by the early 1980s the Seagrams Distilleries was one of the largest makers of liquor in the world. Seagrams is now owned by Bronfman's children and grandchildren, who have inherited his sharp business sense.

Canadian Americans have also excelled in the world of science. When the Royal Swedish Academy of Sciences awarded its 1983 Nobel Prize in chemistry, it looked as though an American had won. But the winner, Henry Taube of Stanford University, was born a Canadian.

Many other former Canadians have made important contributions to the United States and have become well known in both countries. People such as Saul Bellow, the Pulitzer Prize-winning novelist; John Kenneth Galbraith, an economist and adviser to many U.S. presidents; and Richard Tucker, an opera star, all came from Canada. Television news programs feature former Canadians Peter Jennings and Morley Safer. Oscar Peterson, one of the greatest jazz musicians, and Yousef Karsh, a world-famous portrait photographer, both hail originally from Canada.

Many famous actors and actresses in the United States were also born in Canada. Mack Sennett, a silent-movie director famous for his comic movies, especially those starring the Keystone Kops, was a Canadian. Sennett often used actress Marie Dressler in his movies, who was also from Canada. One of the greatest silent-movie stars, Mary Pickford, was so well liked that she was nicknamed "America's Sweetheart." Most people are not aware that she was Canadian-born.

Over the years many Canadian actors have acted the parts of famous Americans. Canadian-American Raymond Massey became known as the best actor ever to play the part of the American president—Abraham Lincoln. Massey played Lincoln in the 1930s play "Abe Lincoln in Illinois." When he first tried out for the part in New York, people did not like the idea of a Canadian playing the part of Abraham Lincoln. In fact, as soon as people found out, the New York *Daily News* ran a story with the headline "A Canadian As Abraham Lincoln?" Americans may not have been sure about Massey at first, but that soon changed. The play was a great success and was later made into a movie. Massey had a long film career after that.

America's most famous television space hero, Captain James T. Kirk, commander of the U.S.S. *Enterprise* on

the series *Star Trek*, was played by William Shatner, who is originally from Montreal. *Star Trek* ran for only three years, but the series has lived on and has thousands of loyal fans.

Canadian stars in Hollywood include Michael J. Fox, star of the hit movie, *Back to the Future*, and the comedian Jim Carrey. Carrey has appeared as a pet detective in the *Ace Ventura* movies and as the Riddler in *Batman Forever*. As a boy growing up in Toronto, Carrey says he spent hours making funny faces in front of the mirror and made his family laugh with his impressions of television stars.

Other famous Canadian entertainers in the United States include the magician Doug Henning. Even the comic book hero Superman was created by a Canadian, Joe Shuster.

While there are many Canadian and Canadian American celebrities, most Canadians and Canadian Americans are hard-working people who make whatever contribution they can to life in Canada and the United States. Canadians are the first to admit that sometimes they stand in the shadow of Americans. This cannot be helped in some ways—there are ten times as many Americans as there are Canadians. But Canadians believe strongly in their own country. They have always worked to be the best at what they do. Canadians are proud that they have helped improve many people's lives around the world, including the lives of Americans. They are indeed good neighbors to the whole world.

Comedian Jim Carrey has starred in the popular Ace Ventura *movies.*

APPENDIX

Canadian Embassy and Consulates in the United States

Canada's consulates and its embassy want to help Americans learn about and understand Canadian customs and people. They can give you much information about the different areas and peoples of Canada and often have brochures and books that can help you plan a trip to Canada.

Washington, D.C.
Canadian Embassy
501 Pennsylvania Ave., N.W.
Washington, D.C. 20001
Phone (202) 682-1740

Atlanta, Georgia
Canadian Consulate General
400 South Tower
One CNN Center
Atlanta, Georgia 30303-2705
Phone (404) 577-6810

Boston, Massachusetts
Canadian Consulate General
Three Copley Pl., Suite 400
Boston, Massachusetts 02116
Phone (617) 262-3760

Buffalo, New York
Canadian Consulate General
One Marine Midland Center
Suite 3150
Buffalo, New York 14203-2884
Phone (716) 852-1247

Chicago, Illinois
Canadian Consulate General
Two Prudential Plaza
180 North Stetson Ave.
Suite 2400
Chicago, Illinois 60601
Phone (312) 616-1860

Dallas, Texas
Canadian Consulate General
St. Paul Place, Suite 1700
750 N. St. Paul Street
Dallas, Texas 75201-3281
Phone (214) 922-9806

Detroit, Michigan
Canadian Consulate General
600 Renaissance Center
Suite 1100
Detroit, Michigan 48243-1704
Phone (313) 567-2340

Los Angeles, California
> Canadian Consulate General
> 300 South Grand Avenue
> 10th Floor California Plaza
> Los Angeles, California 90071
> Phone (213) 687-7432

Minneapolis, Minnesota
> Canadian Consulate General
> 701 4th Ave. S, Suite 900
> Minneapolis, Minnesota 55415-1899
> Phone (612) 333-4641

New York, New York
> Canadian Consulate General
> 1251 Ave. of the Americas
> New York, New York 10020-1175
> Phone (212) 768-2400

Seattle, Washington
> Canadian Consulate General
> 412 Plaza 600
> Sixth and Stewart Streets
> Seattle, Washington 98101-1286
> Phone (206) 443-1777

GLOSSARY

akutaq (AHK oo tahk)—Inuit food made with fish and berries

Bombardier, J. Armand (bohm BAHR dyay jay ahr-MAH[N])—Quebec-born inventor of the snowmobile, or Ski-Doo®

Cabot (KAB ut), **John**—Italian-born explorer who was the first European to visit North America after the Vikings

Cartier, Jacques (KAHR tyay zhahk)—French explorer who first charted the St. Lawrence River

Champlain (sham PLAYN), **Samuel de**—French adventurer who helped explore and settle New France

Chretien, Jean (KREH tee en zhawn)—prime minister of Canada and leader of the Liberal party

Conacher, Lionel (KAHN ah kur LYE nel)—famous all-around Canadian athlete

Craigellachie (KRAYG eh lach ee)—site in British Columbia where the final spike of the Canadian Railway was driven

Diefenbaker (DEEF en bayk ur), **John**—thirteenth Canadian prime minister

Gagnon, Andre (gahn YAHN AHN dray)—French-Canadian musician

Gua, Pierre de (GOO ah pee ER deh)—early French settler of New France

Iglulik (IHG loo lihk)—a tribe of Inuit

Inuit (IHN yoo iht)—the first people to inhabit the northern regions of Canada; *Inuit* means "people."

Inuktitut (ih NUK tih tut)—a common Inuit language

Jeunesses Musicales du Canada (jeh NES myoo zih-KAHL doo KAHN uh duh)—music school for children

koot'yah (koo TCHEE ah)—boiled wheat and honey

lacrosse (luh KRAWS)—game played with a hard rubber ball and sticks with netted heads

Laurentians (law REN shunz)—mountain range located mainly in Quebec

Laurier (LAW ree yay), **Wilfri**—seventh Canadian prime minister

Lévesque, René (lay VEK reh NAY)—founder of the Parti Québécois

L'Ordre de Bon Temps (LOR dreh deh bohn tawn)—French for "The Order of Good Cheer"; a social group organized to help early settlers get through winter

"Maître chez nous" (MAY treh shay noo)—French for "masters in our house"; a slogan used by Quebecers to express their desire to separate from the rest of Canada

Matonabbee (mah TAHN uh bee)—Indian chief who guided explorer Samuel Hearne

Métis (MAY tee)—Canadians descended from fur traders and their Indian wives

Montcalm, Louis Joseph (mahn KAHM loo EE zhoh-SEF)—French commander who lost to the British in the battle of Quebec

Montreal (MAHN tree awl)—an island in the St. Lawrence River and the largest city in Quebec

Nanaimo (nen EYE moh)—city in British Columbia

Netsilik (NET sih lihk)—an Inuit tribe

Nova Scotia (NOH vuh SKOH shuh)—an Atlantic Province

Okanagan (oh keh NAW gun) **Valley**—a fertile region of British Columbia famous for its fruit and vegetables

Papineau (PAH pee noh), **Joseph**—French Canadian who led an uprising in Lower Canada

Parliament (PAHR luh munt)—the lawmaking branch of national government, which includes the House of Commons, the Senate, and the governor-general

Parti Québécois (pahr TEE kay beh KWAH)—a political party of Quebec that called for Quebec's separation from Canada

Pelletier (pel TYAY), **Wilfrid**—Quebec-born musician who worked with the Metropolitan Opera Company of New York

poutine (poo TEEN)—dish of French fries, cheese, and gravy

Quebec (kweh BEK, or kay BEK)—an eastern Canadian province

ragoût de boulettes et de pattes de cochon (rah GOO deh boo LET ay deh PAHT deh COH shawn)—French-Canadian stew made of meatballs and pigs' feet

reciprocity   (res uh PRAHS uh tee)—a free-trade policy

réveillon   (reh VAY yawn)—traditional feast in Quebec after Mass on Christmas

Richler, Mordecai   (RIHCH lur   MOR dee kye)—Canadian author

St. Jean Baptiste   (sahn zhawn bah TEEST) **Day**—June 24; a legal holiday in Quebec

St. Laurent, Louis   (sahn law RAHN loo EE)—twelfth Canadian prime minister

Saskatchewan   (sas KATCH uh wahn)—a Prairie Province

tourquettes   (toor KET)—maple sap poured on snow and rolled into taffy with a stick

tourtiére   (TOR tee air)—traditional French-Canadian meat pie

Trudeau, Pierre   (troo DOH   pee ER) **Elliott**—fifteenth Canadian prime minister

Selected Bibliography

Boulton, Marsha. *Just a Minute: Glimpses of Our Great Canadian Heritage*. Toronto: Little, Brown and Co., 1994.

Canada Yearbook. Ottawa: Publication Sales and Services, Statistics Canada. Published annually.

Cruxton, J. Bradley. *Flashback Canada*. Toronto: Oxford University Press, 1978.

Fowke, Edith. *Folklore of Canada*. Toronto: McClelland and Stewart, 1976.

Garrod, Stan. *Canada—Growth of a Nation*. Toronto: Fitzhenry and Whiteside, 1980.

Hill, Lawrence. *Trials and Triumphs: The Story of African Canadians*. Toronto: Umbrella Press, 1993.

Hocking, Anthony. *The Canada Series*. New York: McGraw-Hill Ryerson, 1978.

Iglotiorte, John. *An Inuk Boy Becomes a Hunter*. Halifax: Nimbus Publishing, 1994.

Langston, Laura. *Pay Dirt: The Search for Gold in British Columbia*. Victoria: Orca Books Publishers, 1995.

Newlands, Anne. *The Group of Seven and Tom Thomson*. Willowdale: Firefly Books, 1995.

Saywell, John. *Canada—Past and Present*. Toronto: Clark, Irwin and Co., 1975.

Smith, Don. *How Sports Began*. New York: Stadia Sports Publishing, 1977.

INDEX

Ontario, 14, 15, 22, 32, 33, 64, 68, 70–71, 109, 126, 130, 134, 156
Ottawa, 6, 15, 23, 24, *25*, *44*, 45, 84, 109
Ottenbrite, Anne, 151

Papineau, Joseph, 61
Pearson, Lester B., 42, 81–83
Pelletier, Wilfrid, 40
Peterson, Oscar, 162–163
Pickford, Mary, 163
Podborski, Steve, 153
political parties, 24, 83, 84
Prairie Provinces, 15, 126
Prince Edward Island, 12, 13, 35, 115, 123

Quebec, 13–14, 23, 32, 37–40, 61, 64, 71, 83–85, 99, 105–106, 124, 134–135, 139, 156: separatist movement, 84–85
Quebec City, 14, 53, 55–58, 105, 106

Raffi, 40
recipes: Arctic Char, 129–130; Nanaimo Bars, 127–129; Wild Rice, 131
Richardson family, 118–120
Richler, Mordecai, 37
Riel, Louis, 70–71
Rupert's Land, 67, 70

Safer, Morley, 162
St. Laurent, Louis, 81
Saskatchewan, 15, 16, *17*, 36, 71, 96, 126
Scott, Thomas, 70, 71
Sennett, Mack, 163
Seven Years' War, 55–58
Shatner, William, 163–165
Shuster, Joe, 165
sports, 45, 145–153: basketball, 145–146, 151, *152*; ice hockey, 45, 137, 145, 147–149, 151; lacrosse, 146–147; Olympics, 151–153; professional teams, 151; school sports, 139; school-yard games, 137; winter sports, 149
Stratford festival, 38

Taube, Henry, 162
Taylor, Ken, 42–43

Tecumseh, 60
Tennant, Veronica, 32
Thompson, David, 59
Toronto, 15, 27, 32, 109
Trudeau, Pierre Elliott, 43, 84–86, 87
Tucker, Richard, 162
Turner, John, 88

Vancouver, 18, *20*, 27, 41, 68
Vikings, 49

wildlife, 15, *16*, 18, 32, 116, 141
Wolfe, James, 56, 58
World War I, 77–78, 103
World War II, 79, 109

Young, Neil, 40
Yukon Territory, 21, 24, 112, 129

ABOUT THE AUTHOR

Adam Bryant has had the chance to get to know both Canada and the United States well. In addition to traveling across both countries, coast to coast, he attended elementary school in New York and college in Canada. These experiences, he says, gave him insights into the differences and similarities that mark Canada and the United States.

In this book, Adam Bryant attempts to portray the many heritages and peoples of the huge country of Canada. He hopes that readers will come to appreciate the rich culture of the Canadian people and the beauty of the Canadian landscape.

Adam Bryant has been a television news writer and television host of *Kidsbeat*, a children's news show, in Toronto. He is now a reporter for *The New York Times*. He and his wife, Jeanetta, and their two daughters, Anna and Sophia, live in Westchester County, New York.